A CLOSED EYE

Though He Slay Me

TAMIKA MARIE

All Scripture quotations are taken from the Holy Bible, King James Version, KJV

Cover by Olivia Cooper, Newport News VA

Prologue

The composition of this book has proven to be the most challenging endeavor I have undertaken to date. I have grappled with the decision of what to disclose to my readers and what to withhold. There have been moments when I contemplated abandoning this project due to feelings of shame and sense of defeat. At times, the emotional weight of revisiting certain experiences felt insurmountable. It was only during a recent journey that I came to the realization that in order for my narrative to resonate globally, I must confront the barriers I have so diligently tried to avoid.

Throughout my life, I have been taught that the Lord will provide all our needs; a truth I wholeheartedly affirm. However, it is essential to recognize that *He* understood that the needs of *His* people would necessitate the assistance of doctors, lawyers, therapists, educators, and various other professionals. He has made available to us the tangible resources required to navigate the complexities of life. In my view, seeking therapy has been the most constructive step I could take towards safeguarding my mental health, complemented by the guidance of the Almighty Lord.

This book serves as a cherished offering to all who have endured tragic events in their lives. If I can preserve, so can you. I implore you not to lose hope. There is a future awaiting you, and there are individuals who depend on your presence. Hold On, because help is on the way!

Present Day

November 5, 2024,

As the ocean moves with a natural grace, its waves receding (like this man's hairline walking across the ocean), and flowing in a rhythm that feels both effortless and timeless. Each wave rises and falls responding to the pull of the moon and the winds not being burdened by the needs of validation or approval. In a similar way, many of us wish to express ourselves freely without the weight of judgment from others.

I find myself in a place of uncertainty on whether I should approve this book to be released, so much so, it has driven me into a state of mental distress. Can you imagine if we could communicate like the ocean moves, fluently and apologetically. We might find a deeper connection a deeper connection within ourselves and those around us. I'm sitting here struggling to ask God for what I need; not wanting the answer because of my desire to do things my way. Why is it so hard to surrender? Why are we so "fleshly" at times? We pray the prayer of "Lord do it for me" but are we ready to succumb to his plan for us.

Though I have concluded that no matter how I feel I am going to complete this assignment, it's hard especially with everything going on in my life. I rest on remembering one of many scriptures, "For ye have not received the spirit of bondage again to fear, but ye have received the spirit of adoption, whereby we cry, Abba, Father" (Romans 8:15). My father, who is in heaven, will be right by my side every step of the way. He promised to never leave me nor forsake me.

Lord, my prayer to you is to send a reminder to me to remind me of what you've done before so I will submit myself wholeheartedly to you. Lord, you said, "that the sufferings of this present time are not worthy to be compared with the glory which shall be revealed in us" (Romans 8:18). Help me God to fulfill my purpose. Lead me and guide me into all understanding.

I think on a well-known scripture which lets us know "all things work together for good to them that love God, to them who are called according to his purpose" (Romans 8:28). I am going to stand firm knowing the weapons of our warfare are not carnal. God will strengthen me with every step I take, with every question asked, with every negative comment presented, and with every judgment made towards me. It is now time to sign my name: *Tamika Marie – author, completed trilogy documents, ready for distribution.*

CHAPTER ONE

How may I be of service to you.........

"To be honest, I am not sure where to start. There are so many thoughts and emotions built up inside that I can't pinpoint the root of all my emotions. I was raised upright. I've had the perfect loving family, no absence. I don't understand how I got to this point in my life, maybe rebellion, curiosity, ignorance, or selfishness. All I have wanted was one thing in life. One simple thing. Children grow up every day with dreams of being a doctor, a lawyer, a celebrity, a millionaire and so forth. As for me.... I just wanted to be loved. I wanted a family (husband, children, dog, house and white picket fence."

Are these things still something you want? I noticed you mentioned "wanted" as in past tense, meaning no more.

"I'm really not sure what I want, and what I want doesn't matter anymore. I have lost so much. I feel like every time I grasp a piece of happiness, it is taken from me. I'm starting to believe I am not meant to be happy anymore. Why is it that I can't have the things that I want? Even the things I need seem so far out of my grasp. Life can't be like this; it just can't be. Lord, please help me."

I felt myself rambling on and on. I was so tired. My eyes mimicked a raccoon, my edges were flying away in every other direction than where they were supposed to be, and my lips were dry. Overall, I looked depressed; nearly homeless. I had no desire to fool with these therapists trying to get in my head. In my eyes, therapists were just like any other doctor who make up any ole diagnosis to keep you coming back. It's as if you're being robbed in plain sight. Yet…..., I was here.

The therapist looked at me with her undivided attention, taking in everything I had said. She looked at me taking in not just the content of what I was saying, but also how I was saying it. She seemed intrigued with my unorganized thoughts and expressions. It was as if every emotion I felt, every hand gesture I'd made, and every wrinkle that pronounced itself on my face, she felt with me. It was reassuring as well as a little bizarre to me. They say a good therapist observes eye contact, facial expressions, posture, and nonverbal cues. So, I guess sis was just doing her job. It still sparked my curiosity of what she thought of me after my wallow of self-pity. Well… No! I really don't care. It's time to go! Where's my purse? I've been here a minute too long and she's not about to charge me extra for this session.

I walked anxiously down the hall, subconsciously telling Mrs. Jane off. "Write down your emotions," she says. Blah! Blah! Blah! When I initially walked in for my session and Mrs. Jane introduced herself as my therapist, I initially thought of Tarzan, "Me Jane, you Tarzan!"

however it goes. I really have to stop watching so many movies.

"Pheobe, get back on track girl, your mind is always wandering," I told myself. I didn't care who was around to see me giving myself a much-needed pep talk. Shoot, they could join the conversation if they'd like.

I headed for the parking garage to start my drive back home. I thought of all the years that had passed. Never in a million years did I think I would be where I am today mentally, physically, emotionally, and financially. It's crazy how life can just pass us by so quickly. I'm thankful to be alive, and so appreciative of everything God has brought me from. I sometimes question what the reasoning is for all that I have endured? Is it purely from disobedience? Or is it just a part of the trials I have to partake in during my time down here on earth? Nevertheless, all is well.

Growing up in church, they taught us that we shouldn't question God, but how can we be real with God if we don't ask questions? How can we build a relationship with him without talking to him and understanding why we are on the path we are on currently or experiencing things we are experiencing without asking questions. My questions are not of disrespect but of curiosity. Is it not his plan for us to grow in him? The way in which others feel we are questioning God is not the manner in which they perceive. We build relationships with others by asking questions, right? Maybe I have the wrong perception, who knows? I have realized over the years that the questions we ask will not always have the answers we seek.

Through all of these questions, I began to realize why Mrs. Jane asked that I purchase and retain a diary. It is to express myself in plain sight and create a better understanding of what I am feeling. I needed to control my emotions and organize my thoughts. A "normal" person has a challenging time wrestling through a whole cluster of emotions, so I knew my mind was screwed up with everything I had been through.

I entered the car and drove to the nearest Target to purchase a journal. I told myself this was just a journal journey and nothing more. Luckily, Denise called me, and I was able to stay on track.

Denise: Hey, bestie! What are you doing?

(*I began to tell her what the therapist had wanted me to do. She thought it was a great idea and agreed to create a journal with me to organize how she was feeling which also made me feel so at ease.*)

I purchased a matching journal for Denise as well and checked out of Target. "This is going to be a great journey," I thought to myself. Maybe this will help me with everything that is going on.

Later that night, I attended church. It was nothing short of amazing considering my plan was to stay home that night. I was extremely tired from waking up early and working late. However, I made a promise to the Lord that I intended to keep.

I've reached a point in my life where I'm tired of falling short; especially when it comes to making the same mistakes over and over again. I've been kind of keeping my distance from a lot of things and people to maintain my peace. This space where I've felt isolated before has become a comfort zone. It's so weird cause I absolutely hated it before. I cried and cried when I was going through it. I felt that I didn't deserve everything that happened to me. Why should I be cut off from the world when I've done nothing wrong? I made the mistakes that I had made, however I never intentionally caused harm or threatened anyone in any way.

I had to learn that people will react in the way they think is best. It is no fault of theirs, it's just how they feel things should be and it's ok. Does that make me or them a bad person? Absolutely not! There is a reason for everything and a season for everything, and no one is better than the other. No one can say how they would react or behave differently unless they are in that specific position. Also, not everyone has the same strengths, structure, or morals as you. I have come to realize that charity is what we can offer one another to keep one another afloat.

What is charity? It is a voluntary offering to assist those in need without selfishness. It is a selfless act of love that is genuine and from the heart. Without charity there is no love.

CHAPTER TWO

I sat in my mustard yellow velvet accent chair in the corner of my bedroom dressed in my robe. It was positioned directly in front of the wall-to-wall bay window to view the morning sunrise and evening sunset. Across the room, sat my queen-sized bed attached to a ceiling high quilted headboard and two nightstands. Adjacent to my bed, sat my dresser, stand up mirror, and a walk-in closet attached to a coupled bathroom with a large soak-in-tub. Finishing my bedroom oasis were natural oak hardwood floors and hanging portraits decorated with shades of gold, yellow, and rose.

I decided to bring out my black diary after thinking about everything Mrs. Jane had shared with me. I knew I was depressed which was something her and I agreed upon. My life felt like a bad case of de ja vu; constantly living similar days over and over again.

"Whelp!" I thought, "let me get to it". No need to keep lingering in my misery.

Dear Diary:

I sit here trying to encourage myself when I have no strength to even place my foot one in front of the other. I'm finding myself in a continuous daze for days. There are moments when people are talking to me, and I don't even hear them. Why am I like this, Lord? Why so much pain? Why do I carry this burden? Why do I question you when I know you have not forgotten about me? We learned in Bible study that God has a remedy for us to get back to him. We are never too far from him. All we have to do is turn to him with our whole heart. We must fast to make our flesh suffer. But ultimately, we have to first acknowledge that we need help. We'll never get what God has for us until we render our hearts to him. If God can use

David who couldn't keep himself and had a man killed to have another man's wife; he can certainly save and use us.

Why did God use me? Why have I been the subject of all this pain I have endured? I know I shouldn't complain because I know there have been so many others in a worse predicament than I am. I just want to know the purpose of all of this. I'm here, at my age, a single mom, and barely making it. Is this the life you have destined for me? If so, I don't understand it, Lord. I don't know why I am here. Why did you save me for me to continue reliving these moments over and over again, it makes no sense to me. I lost a child when I was seventeen and now, I have been completely stripped by a man whom I have loved genuinely. Are you punishing

me? This can't be the life you set up for me. This just can't be. Maybe I deserve this.

The more I began to write in the diary the more frustrated I became. This course of treatment obviously was not helping. I felt horrible for questioning God. I knew better. I stood up, gathered myself, and headed to the bathroom to get ready for work. I had to go to see Mrs. Jane tomorrow and I certainly wasn't excited about it.

Surprisingly, my workday went fast; the day was productive with no difficult clients. I loved working for VOLOL Health Systems; they cared for their employees better than any job I'd encountered in the past. The company offered great benefits and resources to help those who needed it outside of the workplace. I have been with them for about four years already. During this time, I had earned multiple raises. The work hours were even great, which allowed me to be the mom I needed to be.

LWRACC Youth Choir rehearsal was tonight, and I sure needed to go. I was always raised in the church; however, I was never heavily involved, as I am at LWRACC. It was an amazing feeling and space where I didn't have to think or worry about what was going on in my life. My thoughts were clear here.

We began with a prayer and warm up, then dove right into the song selections chosen for that Sunday. We started to rehearse, and something just began to lift inside of me. I knew I wasn't the only one feeling the way I felt, because the whole atmosphere shifted.

We all stood up to completely run through the songs. By the time we finished all the songs, tears were rolling down my face and that of others. Something was stirring up inside and I just couldn't hold it in anymore, so I began crying and worshipping. Faintly, I could hear others crying and worshipping with me. The spirit of the Lord shifted through and all I could shout out is GLOORRAYY! Before I knew it, I was on the other side of the church completely full of praise. When I was finally able to get back to my seat, I noticed that everyone was scattered around in complete worship. No matter how often I tried to calm myself down, I just couldn't. It's amazing how God will show up and give you just what you need when you need it. I gathered my things and returned home to get ready for my morning routine. Adulthood = the same thing over and over again each day; especially when kids are involved. I loved each and every moment of it though.

My appointment with Mrs. Jane was early that morning, and I had to make sure I had everything I needed in order to allow myself to have a smooth transition throughout the day. Mornings are not my thing; I struggle daily when it comes to getting up bright and early. However, somehow, working mornings was the best fit for my busy life. After my appointment, I would go straight to work. I made sure I had my diary with me to discuss with Mrs. Jane, and I wondered if this visit would be better than my initial one.

The next morning, I woke up fully rested. I made sure everything was in order, grabbed my black book, and left the house. "Today, is going to be an amazing day", I thought to myself. I said a quick prayer before pulling out of the driveway to make it to Mrs. Janes by 9 am.

I pulled into the parking lot feeling a bit nervous. I grabbed my iced caramel latte with EXTRA caramel drizzle from the Local Pop & Shop and switched into the building. "Good morning are you checking in for an appointment?" the receptionist asked. "Yes ma'am," I answered and gave her my name before she directed me to have a seat until I was called. I decided to keep the foolery going and switched to my seat before plopping down in the chair obnoxiously.

CHAPTER THREE

Mrs. Jane invited me back to her room for our session. The small talk during the long walk to her office seemed like an eternity. I was ready to get this session done and over with.

Momentarily I became distracted by the dull, moss-covered walls leading into her office. It seemed strange I hadn't noticed it before. Its tone was uneven creating an unpleasant, almost impulsive visual.

We entered the room silently. I sat foolishly in the seat flipping my fingers around one another contemplating whether I wanted to let her in on how I have felt for the last several years. It was easy to make the call for help, however, opening up was a whole different story.

"Pheobe," Ms. Jane said. I distractedly replied, "Yes". She looked over at me with her glasses resting on top of her nose with her wrist resting on the bottom of her chin "How have you been since our last session?", she said. I looked back at her shyly and before I knew it, I was talking:

"Ms. Jane, if I must be honest, I'm really nervous about going through all of these sessions and still feeling the same way. I've been stuck in this space of uncertainty and shame, and. I don't know how much more of it I can take. I've been too scared to tell people what's going on with me concluding that they would look at me funny or want nothing to do with getting to know me. I've had a challenging time building relationships in fear of being judged and or bringing the same hurt into another relationship. Ms. Jane, I'm really just all over the place. I just want to get better and be better overall. One shouldn't have to live their lives managing so much."

Ms. Jane looked back at me with a smile, waved her hand forward to cue me to continue.

"I did the journaling. The first entry may have been a little blunt toward this process just because I am a bit skeptical about how this is all going to *pan* out. But overall, I enjoyed writing in my little black journal."

Ms. Jane nodded her head in acceptance. She slid in her chair to reposition herself to cross her legs: *"Pheobe, I want you to know I am going to do my absolute best to assist you in what you are going through. Very few people have survived what you've been through. I can only imagine how traumatic it has been for you throughout the years. I have been counseling for years and feel I can really help you in your journey to realizing your self-worth. However, I just need you to be committed like I am. I would also like you to also consider going to our group therapy sessions. It's a confidential service we offer to ladies such as yourself who have also been through traumatic experiences. I feel hearing others' stories will allow you room to understand that you are not alone. There is no need to feel that people are judging you or let alone embarrassed about what you've been through. There are genuine people around who just want to be there for you. Building relationships is good, especially healthy ones of course. What do you think about everything I just said Pheobe?"*

My eyes were in a bubble of tears. I was trying my best not to blink so the tears wouldn't fall down my face. I was tired of crying. They say crying helps to heal; I would argue the contrary. I nodded to Ms. Jane, agreeing with everything she said as I grabbed a tissue from the tissue box adjacent to my arm. I wiped my tears and accepted her offer to attend the group therapy sessions. Afterall, it didn't seem like a bad idea. Maybe hearing the stories of others will help me heal as well. Maybe my story would help someone heal. It's worth a try.

I continued wiping my eyes with the tissues from the desk aside me when Ms. Jane asked me if I could tell her how all this began.

Before I knew it, I found myself talking to Ms. Jane like we'd been best friends for years. At this point, I trusted her. I mean, after all, legally she wasn't allowed to tell anyone what I was talking to her about unless it is detrimental to my safety or that of another's. In my eyes, I was safe.

"I met Jonah after about two years working at McDonalds. I was about five to six months pregnant when he was hired there. He would flirt with me so much. Mrs. Jane, I'm not going to lie though, I was feeling him. He had greenish hazel eyes with a smile that lit up his entire face. His tint of caramel skin and perfect white teeth attracted me even more. He was clean, well built, and hard working. I just figured with all the flirting he was doing he was being funny in front of his boys. You know how guys are in front of their friends. Considering I was pregnant, I mean full blown pregnant, why would he really be interested in me. One night at a bowling event for the employees, Jonah finally approached me seriously stating how he wanted to be with me. I asked him did he see my stomach, and he stated he didn't care. He even went on to state how he would take care of my child and me. I expressed the importance of being independent, which was how my father had raised his girls. He smiled and said, "OK". From there, I guess you can say, everything else is history.

After beginning to tell her about how I met Jonah, Ms. Jane brought up the group therapy sessions she had previously recommended I attend. I assured her I was still interested in moving forward with whichever treatment she thought was best for me. Ms. Jane scheduled a follow up appointment for the following week and handed me a flyer which consisted of the location and directions to the where the group therapy sessions are held.

The ride home was such a relief. I couldn't wait for Brenda to call so I could tell her what occurred at my session today. She agreed it would be beneficial for me to attend therapy to sort out everything I've been going through. She felt it would help me to heal properly. It's crazy how one may think they have healed from their past; only to find out that there is still pain lurking deep down inside of them.

My group session was in a few days. I kept going back and forth in my thoughts about what I would and would not share. "Maybe I'll meet someone whose been through the same things I have," I thought. The more I thought about it the better I began to feel about group therapy.

CHAPTER FOUR

Sundays provide me with significant emotional, physical, and spiritual relief. Attending church each week allows me to let go of the stresses of life. There's something truly special about stepping into a sanctuary where I feel relaxed and at home; it's my place of healing. However, I often find that as soon as I leave, the worries of the world can creep back in, which is frustrating. There are days when I wish I could just stay.

During the service, the bishop delivered a powerful sermon on "Second Chances." He asked us, "What are you going to do with you second

chance?" He even shared a large poster
that appeared to be a summary from a doctors
visit, holding it up for the congregation to see:

*This is the paperwork from my doctor. These are
the visits that I've had and the medications that I should
be taking. Every medication that they tell me I should be
taking for the conditions going on with the heart and the
liver and the kidneys and the pancreas and the prostate.
Everyone they recommend, I say God is going to do it. I
haven't taken the medication yet. I'm trusting God. I don't
want to talk about God being a healer and then I don't
depend on him to heal. My symptoms were saying one
thing, but God is saying something else. The Bible says,
"Write the Vision and make it plain, upon tables that he
may run that readeth it" (Matthews 2:2).*

He proceeded to express his fearlessness
in sharing what the Lord has done for him. He
pulled out multiple summaries from his doctor
visits and asked one of the deacons to read the
report aloud. The deacon read each biopsy result,
revealing that EVERYTHING WAS BENIGN!!

The erupted in worship, celebrating the joy of the Lord. Bishop then quoted Isaish 43, which beautifully assures us of God's presence and protection:

1. "But now thus saith the Lord, that created thee, O Jacob, and he that formed thee, O Israel, Fear not: for I have redeemed thee, I have called thee by thy name; thou art mine.

2. When thou passes through the waters, I will be with thee; and through the rivers, they shall not overflow thee: when thou walkest through the fire, thou shalt not be burned, neither shall the flame kindle upon thee." He then proceeds on with his sermon to state:

The great creator, the one who made you is in control. Don't you dare lay in your bed one more night and worry about how God is going to bring you out? You already got the victory a long time ago. God gave you the victory before he formed you in your mother's womb. He knew the ending at the beginning. It might be a whole lot of people in your life who might have rejected you. Who might not want you around. But guess what? Goodbye, baby! As long as I belong to God, I'm all right. If you belong to Jesus Christ you belong to the chief physician, the great deliverer, you belong to the way maker. So, what you got to be sad about? He will be with you. When you're getting your MRI, he'll be with you! When you are going through your divorce, he'll be with you! When your children walk away from you, he'll be with you! Know that when you go through the waters, he'll be with you! The world and your situation will cause you to believe that God is not with you. Because you're going through something, but you have to walk by faith and not by sight. And know that God will never leave you nor forsake you. God is right there! That means when you go through the rivers. Just because you get through this week does not mean something will not come up next week. Though you go through the waters, they shall not overflow you. You're not going to go under just because trouble comes your way. It's coming but it's not going to take you under. That's why folks look at you trying to figure out after all the H E double hockey sticks you've been through, how you are still standing. I'm still standing because God would not let this mild problem that

I have overtaken me. Because he is still with me.

There are going to be some situations that you can't avoid, but Jesus said while you're walking through the fire you shall not be burned. Amen. Just like the children, the three boys, who were tossed into the fire. Amen. The fire did not burn them. I want you to know that the enemy is trying to put a whole lot of us in the fire. Amen. He wants us to believe that because we see the fire and we smell the fire; that the fire is going to overtake us. Just because you see something does not mean what you see is going to overtake you. Amen. You shall not be burned. It shall not overtake you. It shall not trouble you. Amen. Amen. Neither shall the flame kindle you. I need somebody in this house to understand that the enemy cannot get you because God has a hedge all around you. The hedge of protection that God has around you is because he loves you and you belong to him. I've seen too much now. I've been through too much now. I never thought that I would live past the age of twenty-seven. Amen. I've been kidnapped twice. Amen. I hung out in places I shouldn't have. I come out of the crack house, but he gave me a second chance so I'm depending on God. God brought me too far not to trust him. He has brought me too far for me not to believe in him. I believe what the word says. If I die let me die. I believe everything God has for me.

The enemy wants you to not believe in God and die. He wants your hope to die, your desires to die, and your ambitions to die. But the devil is a liar. Amen. My situation does not dictate my walk with God. I don't serve God based on how I feel. I serve God based on the word he says. Whatever God says that's it!

God told me that he was going to heal me. I said God how are you going to do it. I said God are you punishing me for my past. You know we ask questions sometimes; God why did you allow me to go through this? He said, "Shut up! and just go through it" and Imma do just want the Lord says. I am redeemed now and because God gave me a second chance, Imma do what I gotta do. Do what you gotta do while you can do it. As long as I live, I shall do what I have to do in my life. God is number uno in my life.

Obedience brings blessings. For the Bible says, "If you be willing and obedient ye shall eat the good of the land". Redeemed, to be freed from captivity by payment or ransom, to be released from blame for a debt, to be freed from the consequences of sin. Redeemed is to be repaired, restored, and retrieved. Your past does not dictate your future. Because when God redeemed you from the hand of the enemy, he gives you a brand-new start; another opportunity for you to love him. Everything that I got wrong yesterday, I can get it right today.

Many times, we'll spend more time wondering about what we lost. We spend hours thinking about what we lost. Instead of taking an opportunity that God has given us to LIVE think about what we can gain. We will find ourselves stuck living in losses. But God is giving us an opportunity to gain. You've got the greatest gift you can have… LIFE! I need you to think about what you're going to do with your life. Are you going to stay at home and just hold the pain and cry about the pain? Or are you going to get up and move with the pain and say the Lord will take care of me? You have to keep on whether there is pain or not. Cause after a while, by faith, God will move the pain. Why do you give up just because it's a pain there, SO WHAT! You're still here! My trust is in the Lord. It's all in God's hand; in his timing. God has not forgotten you. I believe in this season. God is about to do something supernatural for those who keep putting God first. All of

We worshipped deeply, and I found the message profoundly moving. It made me reflect on the pain I had been holding onto and the tears I had shed over situations that no longer served me. I decided that it was time to let go—no more holding on to that hurt. I came to understand that my obedience could create space for new possibilities. I believe that when God speaks, He is true to his word.

CHAPTER FIVE

I pulled into the parking lot of a three-story cement colored building. It was a fairly new building, located on a corner lot, attached to a UPS and storage facility. I walked into the double-sided glass doors to check in at the front desk; the lady at the desk directed me to a conference room furnished with chairs and two tables. The table closest to the door had pamphlets of helpline contacts and different programs for women. I walked slowly past the table glancing over to see if there was anything in which I'd be interested. About six feet down past the end of the pamphlet table, were the refreshments assorted with tags. There was even a coffee and tea bar that shared a table with cookies, chips, crackers, and donuts. All it needed was some ice cream and this would have been my type of gathering.

A middle-aged, dark skinned, well-shaped woman with pretty long black hair began addressing the room. Everyone began to walk towards her to take a seat in a circle. I noticed many of the women looked like me. In fact, we seemed to all be in the same age group. The addressee asked if we could all go around the room and say our first name. She started by telling us her name is Veronica. We all greeted her as if we were in an AA meeting. Many of the women had attended for a few weeks now while the others she welcomed into the group.

I sat quietly observing the group. We each had to then state something unique about ourselves; every woman seemed so interesting but me. There were women who you could tell were still dealing with some situations and others who seemed to be at the end of their healing process.

Then, there was me, who loved to fake the funk, smiling as if I had it all figured out. I shared with the group how I started drafting a book about the experiences that I had faced throughout the years. Surprisingly, they all became so intrigued by what I had to say. When I noticed the attention, I closed my mouth to silence myself and allow someone else to pick it up.

After all the introductions had been made, Veronica cited the rules and mannerism in which we all shall uphold. She explained the importance of confidentiality inside the room as well as outside of the group sessions. She felt it was important for everyone to trust one another for this group to be successful. Veronica argued that is would be of everyone's best interest if they didn't feel even a glimpse of the betrayal we had already faced previously. Afterall, we trusted our partners with our hearts and look what the outcome of that was.

There were about twelve women in the group. My goal wasn't to make friends, just to heal.

The session was over in about an hour. I grabbed my bag from the floor and tried to walk quickly out the door when three other women approached me. They wanted to know more about the book I was writing and asked if I could tell their stories as well. I felt my face frown up obnoxiously with confusion. "I thought Veronica said we would have to keep our stories confidential within the group," I said to the ladies. I remembered their names were Danielle, Tatianna, and Octavia. Danielle looked at me and replied, "Girl, we are asking you to! We just want to help other women as well. We can double check with Veronica to make sure it is ok if you like?" "Yes, please," I said. The Lord knows I didn't want anything to fall back on me. I was going through enough already.

The Girls asked me if I wanted to grab drinks with them. I told them I didn't drink, but I would be happy to go out to eat with them in a more conservative setting. They agreed and we headed out to the Longhorn down the street.

I really didn't have much of an appetite. My mind was settled on going home, bathing, and cuddling up under my pillows and heated blanket. However, deep down, I knew these girls needed me just as much as I needed them. Relationships, why are we made to have them?

We met at Longhorn, ordered our beverages, and began a brief introduction of who we were. Danielle has three children and was recently married. She was short and Hispanic with a sassy but shy demeanor. Tatianna has five children and is divorced. She was also short, light-skinned, curvy, and classy but down to earth. Octavia, on the other hand, was tall. She is a single mother of twins in a long-distance relationship. You could tell by her unique hip clothing arrangement that she loved to party. She was colorful with lots of life in her. To see her, you would never know that she had gone through anything. I tried the relationship thing; clearly it wasn't working for me. I thought it best to be by myself until the Lord sees fit for something else for me.

We had a wonderful time. They each had started their group sessions around the same time. They said they are twice a week. Some of the girls talk on the phone and hang out for extra support throughout the week. I was trying to figure out how they had enough time to attend two meetings cause I barely had the time let alone the energy to attend one.

We finished dinner and agreed to go out again the next week after our meeting. My next session with Ms. Jane was that Wednesday. I told her I enjoyed my first group session and how I went out to dinner with three ladies from the group. She thought it was a good that I went out to dinner with them. In fact, she believed hanging with the ladies is a healthy way to start building healthy relationships again.

I had not mentioned the whole book thing to Ms. Jane until now. She was excited about it. I mentioned how Veronica who was head of the meeting groups said it was ok for me to write Danielle's, Tatianna's, and Octavia's story with a written consent form as well as their approval on what I write before I submit my book. The Girls had agreed that I could share their stories from the sessions. If Veronica were down for it, I guess I couldn't say no. I admired their bravery for even trusting me to draft their stories. Ms. Jane seemed overly excited about this visit. She felt I was on the right path to making progress. She asked me when my next group session was; I told her tomorrow. We ended our session with her reminding me to make sure I'm completing my journal entries. I told her I would make an entry tonight before I went to bed. She nodded and walked me to the front door of the building.

CHAPTER SIX

Dear Diary:

The group sessions have been beneficial thus far. I feel a sense of comfort hearing the other ladies talk about their life stories. Though each of them is in different stage of the healing process, we each share a piece of one another.

I spoke to Jonah today for the first time in about a year. In the past, he texts me a few times as well as video called with short conversations. I assumed he was doing better since the conversation between us was going well. I told him about the book I had finished. He asked what it was about and of course I was completely honest and told him it was about him. He didn't seem to mind at all. He told me I looked good remembering the last time he saw me in person I was 243 pounds. Now, I was sitting at a good 132 pounds.

In a recent conversation, he asked if he could have another chance. I knew he had a girlfriend with a baby on the way. I told him because of how things went for us, I didn't think it would work out between us. We tried, and tried, and tried, over again. It always ended in a bad space. I was in a good place, and I knew getting back involved with him was not what I needed in my life. I loved Jonah, but our time had run its course. I needed no more drama from him. He played me too many times.

My answer must not have been what he wanted to hear, because all of a sudden, he began to get irate. He proceeds to say he made me into the person I am today, and that without him I would be nothing. He went as far as to say that my "leader" was not leading me to the right God; implying that his teachings were misleading which were clouding my head. Of course, I began to defend my Bishop because I knew what he was teaching was straight from the word of God. He continued on and on about "my leader" and how I was nothing. I held back every tear I could. I thought after all these years that he would never have this type of effect on me anymore. I was tired of him telling me how I knew I felt deep down inside. Eventually, I hung the phone up. His words from the present and past began to

I felt myself getting anxious and weary. As I went to shut my journal, I could see small drops of water beginning to make a pattern on my entry. I had no idea I was even tearing. I didn't want to feel this way. I felt so scared. I knew I had nothing to fear, but somehow past feelings were surfacing. I immediately kneeled down beside my bed and began to pray.

When I opened my eyes, it was morning. I had fallen asleep praying. I felt so bad even though I knew it was just the Lord comforting me. I got up from the floor showered and began my devotions. My sister had purchased a "Single Moms Devotions" book for me as a Mother's Day gift. At first, I was a bit skeptical about reading it. The first few pages of the book seemed to be so original. I decided to give it a chance. After a few more days, the daily devotions became inspiring. The daily challenges to complete every day were cultivating.

I completed my mommy duties before I headed to the door to walk to the local coffee shop. Even though I slept so well on my room floor last night, I needed my daily coffee regime.

The weather was perfect this morning, The trees were whistling gently giving off a cool wind which traveled down my spine. The air was crisp and clean, making my walk more relaxing. As I reached the coffee shop, a tall, dark-skinned man held the door waiting for me to enter. He was sculpted well. His muscles were just well defined, peaking my way through his polo shirt. I quickly walked past trying not to make eye contact. I could feel myself blushing, and I did not like it at all. It had been nearly six years since I've been with Jonah. He's the only man I really knew. After our breakup, I just focused on being a mom and school. Until now, no man had ever made me feel so strangely except Jonah.

I stood in line trying to make sure I was taking deep breaths. I felt like a dog that just finished going on his morning run. This line was taking forever today. Maybe, because this fine specimen of a man was behind me.

Finally, it was my turn to order. "Hi, how can I help you today," the cashier said. "Could I have an iced caramel latte with caramel drizzle please and a medium serving will do", I said as I struggled to pull my wallet from my oversized handbag. There was no reason I should be acting this way. It is childish! How can I be embarrassing my own self right now?

I paid, grabbed my drink, and turned slowly to head to the door. I exhaled when I saw he was not there. I went to push the door open, and my face completely flushed. He grinned in my face. I knew he knew I was trying to avoid him. The grin on his face proved so. I knew my cheeks and ears were pink as well. I thanked him for holding the door for me and proceeded on my

way to head back home. "Miss!" I heard from a distance. "Oh, my Lord! I know, he is not calling me!!," I said under my breath with a light stomp. Quickly putting a smile on my face, I turned to face him. He was closer than I thought. By this time, my hands and feet were sweating. He walked straight up to me looking down at me. My knees began to give out. "Lord, get this man away from me," I was saying as softly as I could. "I'm Nathan," he uttered. Did I ask him what his name was, No! "Hi Nathan. I'm Pheobe. How are you?" I said.

Nathan: If I made you feel uncomfortable back at the coffee shop, I apologize. You kind of caught me off guard a bit which doesn't really happen. I'm not trying to waste your time. I just wanted to apologize. Well… and to see if there was a chance we could have coffee here this Saturday.

This man is going to get me in trouble. He not only apologized, which he didn't have to do. But he asked me for coffee. Not a date, just coffee. I have never been on an official date

before. Jonah and I were high school sweethearts. We didn't do dates. We were broke. I agreed to meet Nathan at the coffee shop Saturday. If I had something planned Saturday morning, I certainly wasn't doing it anymore.

Octavia, Danielle, and Tatianna were already sitting down when I arrived for therapy. I brought my notebook to write notes about Tatianna's story tonight. Veronica was aware and present to monitor the note taking. We started the meeting as usual introducing ourselves just in case there were any newcomers in the group. Tonight, it looked to be about the same crowd. Veronica looked at me and asked if I felt comfortable sharing my backstory. She told me I could give as little or as much as I wanted to share. I agreed.

My story, I guess you could say, started in high school. I had met this boy who was such a charmer. He treated me like a queen. There were times where I thought he was a bit jealous, but it was nothing serious that would make me feel unsafe. We hung out a lot and even went to

prom together. Shortly after I graduated; he had to remain to finish his senior year. He was younger than me of course. Things became a little bit rough for him and he dropped out of school. Mrs. Pat, who was one of his teachers, adored him, and with my support, decided she would teach him at night so he could get his diploma. A few years later we moved in together and I became pregnant with our son, Trevor. That's when things really began to fall apart.

I stopped there thinking that would be enough for tonight. From the look of the glares, I knew everyone wanted me to continue on:

Jonah, Trevor's' father, became upset that I didn't want to take him where he wanted to go. He was strung out on drugs and wanted to use my car. I didn't feel comfortable doing so, so he began to push me out of the car while riding into the driveway of our home. He reached over while I was driving to open the door and pushed me out of the car to the ground. I had no shoes on due to my feet swelling from the pregnancy. It was cold that night as well.

The heat was perfect in the car, so I had taken my jacket off. It was early October so one day it would be hot, then the next it was freezing cold.

Jonah moved over to the driver seat and pulled off while I got up from the ground. I had no house keys, and his mother wasn't answering the front door to let me in. I called her on her cell with the little battery I had left, and she still wasn't answering. I began to walk to my parents' house, which was about a fifteen-minute drive, and a forty-five-minute walk, when I heard a big bang. I called my sister, Victoria, to come pick me up. She agreed right as my phone went dead. By the time I reached the front of the street, Victoria was there and so was my car. Jonah had crashed my car into a tree. The windows were shattered, the air bags deployed, and my car was smoking. Not even a minute later, we could hear sirens approaching. Victoria informed me she had called the police due to the nervousness in my voice. She expressed that I was pregnant, and she didn't want to take any chances with me being in harm's way.

The police arrived and began to ask me a million questions to which I didn't clearly know the answers to. In the midst of one of the questions all I could hear was a gunshot and I fell to my knees. The police officers began to call for back up. I opened my eyes hesitantly as Victoria lift me from my knees. The paramedic took me to the hospital for evaluation. Tori followed; knowing I would need a ride home.

It was amazing to me how I was so concerned for the safety of Jonah. Whatever he was smoking completely took over his mind that night. He's had his share of tempers, however, the way he acted tonight was completely uncalled for. I was in such disbelief that he would put his own child at risk.

Victoria came into the room a few moments after my arrival at the hospital. The paramedics were able to take me straight back for the nurses to begin monitoring the baby. Tori let me know that the police officers were still looking for Jonah. They had no insight as to what occurred in the woods. They just knew either someone was shot or merely playing around with a gun to scare off the action that was occurring outside of the woods. I didn't care what was going on I just wanted Jonah to be ok.

After a full workup, I was released from the hospital. I had no injuries. Just minor scrapes and bruises. My parents weren't aware of what happened just yet. Facing Glenn and Marie would be something I knew I soon would have to do. I knew my dad was going to flip for sure. We had our differences, but he loved me dearly.

Days later, I had received a collect call. To my surprise it was Jonah. The police officers had finally caught up to him. He begged me to come down to the courthouse and drop the charges against him. I asked him why he did what he did to me. With ease, he informed me that he didn't remember. He went on to explain how he didn't want to have this conversation over the phone. From that statement, I knew he had remembered what he did. He just chose to lie in order to make himself sound good on the phone; or should I say sound innocent. I told him that I would go to the courthouse the next day to try and get the charges dropped on his behalf. Apparently, that wasn't good enough. He insisted I go at once so he can get out of jail.

I asked him how he thought I was able to go in such a hurry with no CAR!! He crashed that! I would have to find a ride; considering at this point everyone knew what had occurred. He huffed and puffed on the phone

insisting I make it happened. I rolled my eyes at his remark. He had the nerve to rush me for something he did. All of this could have been avoided if he hadn't behaved the way he did toward me.

I had no clue as to how I was going to get to the courthouse. I knew for sure Tori wasn't going to take me. She knew too much about what had happened. She was there when the police were questioning me and saw firsthand what he had done to my car. The crazy part was that he had previously damaged my car twice. One time he knocked the driver's window out, because I wouldn't allow him to use my car. Then, the next time he knocked all the windows out of my car because I threatened to leave him. Both times I took him back. Both times he didn't pick up a single dime to assist me in paying the deductible I owed to get my car back from the collision center.

I should have left the first time he did it that year, but I was young, and I was sure I was in love.

Everyone's eyes were still on me. I thought I had spoken too much. Obviously, this was like a live gossip session that each of the ladies were intrigued with. One of the girls asked if she could ask me a question. I agreed of course. She asked, "Who are you?" It wasn't insulting to me at all. Everyone here knew each other and knew somewhat of everyone's survival story here. I took no offense to what she said. I simply replied, "I am a Domestic Violence Survivor. I have experienced more than most and I have experienced less than most. I am a Survivor, and I am here." The group clapped and we took a brief break to gather ourselves. I had multiple women ask me if I was going to tell the rest of my story, they wanted to know just how bad it got. They said they've had friends and family members who didn't make it out. These ladies were so anxious to know my story and how I SURVIVED!

CHAPTER SEVEN

It was now Tatianna's turn to give her story. I sat with my legs crossed and pen in hand ready to jot down notes from her story. I was anxious, I knew little to nothing about everyone. Veronica opened up the session by introducing Tatianna to the group. Tatianna waved to everyone and began to speak:

We tried to renew our vows on our 10-year anniversary to restart the relationship. Dwight agreed that this marriage was something that he wanted to work on with me. We started fresh trying to mend the pieces that had been broken. Time went on and Dwight just couldn't remain faithful. Dwight would say he was at work, meanwhile, he was with other females. I remember the night when I was searching all over for him, because I had a newborn and I just did not feel well. I called him over and over again trying to tell my husband to get home so I could go to the emergency room. There was an app I had on my phone where I can track where my car was. When I tracked my car, I pulled up behind him driving with a female in the passenger seat. I immediately started beeping the horn and Dwight pulled over. He stepped out of the car to explain that the girl was just a friend. I reasoned with him about how he would feel if I said I was at work, and he saw me with another male. Furthermore, if it's just a friend why not answer the phone and talk to me to let me know what's going on? I know marriage is not about his or hers but ours, but I found that to be very disrespectful. We argued and argued that night. It became so bad Dwight punched holes in the walls of the house, tore the closets out their frame, and threw the TV across the room. My children were so scared and so was I. It didn't matter how much I would try to reason with him, he would make it seem as if it was always my fault. Don't get me wrong. I have not always been the easiest person to get along with. However, I loved him and in return all I got was called names, furniture broken, pinned in corners and so forth. When I tried to tell him, I was going to leave him, he took my car to his cousin house. I pulled up on him again only for his reaction to include breaking all the doorknobs on the car and knocking all my windows out. I couldn't understand how someone could treat me like this. I've cooked for him, encouraged him, stuck by his side through his unfaithfulness, had three of his kids, and he couldn't give me the decency to treat me like I needed to be treated.

Spiritually, Dwight grew up in a Baptist religion. He was not quite understanding of my Apostolic background. I was wrong for thinking that I could change him. As much as I tried to take him to church to hear the word being spoken, he would just come home, blast secular music, and continue to drink recklessly. He would always argue that him and God had their own relationship. He said they were cool. No matter how many times I tried to explain where I was coming from, he agreed temporarily, and continued on to what he wanted to do. We collided with the upbringing of our children as well. There were times when I've tried to devote my time to God, and he would purposely continue in his ways to distract me.

Financially, he was so "unbalanced"! I supported him our whole marriage. I continued to give him money and he would max my credit cards out. Even when I helped him strive to reach the position he is currently in today, he belittled me when he began to make more than me. He was making more money, but I was the one paying bills. We've had both our water and electricity cut off for days. I had to reach out to my parents to assist me, which was extremely embarrassing.

Finally, I couldn't take the lies, the cheating, the yelling, the breaking things, and the temper tantrums anymore. I deserved better. It took a while, but he finally moved out about two years ago. There were times when I was scared to come home because of his reactions or state of mind. I never knew what side of Dwight I would get.

Moving forward, I feel like I will ensure that whomever I build a relationship with will have good morals, is equally yoked, and have the same goals in life. I have to put God first at this point. That's the only way I am going to continue to prosper. I wish I could have waited till I was a little older and mature to get married. My thoughts of "I could change a man" clearly did not work. I want my partner to be more in tuned with Christ. I need him to lead in every way possible.

Today, I am at peace. I'm both excited and scared to see what my future is going to bring. I would not maintain a relationship with Dwight if it weren't for the kids. It was just too toxic. Though I have forgiven him, I feel we couldn't be friends with everything that has happened and how he responds to this day about "peaceful co-parenting." I don't know what the future may bring, but for now, it's a solid NO.

Everyone clapped for Tatianna. I felt like Veronica sitting there taking notes and processing everything that was said. These ladies had a lot of courage talking about their past. It's hard to open up to complete strangers, especially in this type of setting. This group was a nonjudgemental group. There were no smirks, rolling of the eyes, grins, or anything when someone spoke. Everyone was

supportive. I was happy Ms. Jane sent me here.

It was time to go. The girls and I decided to go to the Waffle House. I told them about how

I met Nathan and had plans to meet him this Saturday for coffee. They were laughing at how I described him. We ended the night talking about our goals. I told Octavia, Danielle, and Tatianna I would be creating a vision board for my future. I was tired of "winging life" so to say. It was time I set hard and soft goals for myself. I knew my cousin Brenda had invited me to attend a group event to create a vision board on our IPADS which I planned to attend. The girls loved the idea; they told me to share what I learned from the class with them so they could create a board for themselves. I loved how positive and supportive they were. I had lost a lot of friends because of Jonah. I was finally living again; finally discovering my purpose. I was discovering who Pheobe is! I was ready for whatever. There's one thing I have now that I didn't have before because of my lack of obedience; the Lord. These girls saw something different in me to even allow me to write about them. The sky was the limit. This is my WINNING season!

CHAPTER EIGHT

I decided to call Ms. Jane to set up a session. I had to tell her everything that was going on. I was so excited about how my life was going.

We scheduled our session for Tuesday morning at our usual time. I took the day off of work to figure out what I was going to wear for my coffee date tomorrow morning, I'm sure I was overthinking everything. Nathan seemed like such a gentleman. It seemed weird he didn't have anyone in his life. Maybe he did, and he just needed something extra. Whatever the reason was, there was something about him I just couldn't shake. He was easy on the eyes of course, but his gentle demeanor I had never seen before.

Saturday came and I was so nervous. The babysitter had arrived. I gave her all the instructions while heading out the door. Of course, I was running late. Typical women; just can't be on time.

On the way to the coffee shop, I practiced my responses. I felt dumb. Like for real, was I really carrying on like this at my age? He gets what he gets; I'm not changing who I am or how I interact with anybody. I held my head high and continued my drive down the road into the parking lot of the coffee shop. Normally, I would just walk. But just in case he had some weird vibes going on, I wanted to make sure I had a quick exit plan back home. No games were being played here. For his safety, I was hoping he came "correct" pursuing me.

I decided to write an entry in my journal before heading in to meet him. It was about three minutes after. I still had seven minutes to keep him waiting. "Anticipation should occupy him for some time," I thought. I pulled out my journal to begin my entry:

Dear Diary:

I'm going through a bunch of mixed emotions today. I feel happy but also depressed. My past just won't let me be. It's been years and I seem to not heal. I feel like I'm still in chains. I feel like I don't matter. I feel like I shouldn't be here. The only thing that seems to keep me here is fear of going to hell if I commit suicide. I'm tired of going through triggers. I'm tired of people wondering why I am so timid. I'm tired of not being able to be touched, because everyone is going to hurt me. I have no trust. Yes, my trust resides in the Lord. For I know his word states that he will never leave me nor forsake me (Hebrews 13:5). I fear what I may do to myself. I fear letting someone in just to be hurt. All I keep hearing Ms. Jane tell me is "everyone is not him." How do I know that? Lord why am I ok one day and then the next I'm a wreck. How is it that I don't trust myself to make the right decisions in life when Proverbs 3:5-6 tells me to "Trust in the Lord with all thy heart;

*and lean not unto thine own understanding." Lord, help
me....*

I began to transition into prayer:

*Lord, help me understand what it is you want me
to do. You have given me your word and commandments. I
sit here in fear for my life. I feel I have no purpose. I feel I
have no strength to continue on. I feel I have no being. I am
not okay Jesus. Please help me! Please!*

I lifted my head to a knock on my
window, it was Nathann. I found a great parking
spot right in front of the restaurant. I pressed the
window button on my car to let down the
window. Nathan peaked his head in and asked if I
was ok; I nodded yes. He then asked if he could
sit in the car with me. Hesitantly, I unlocked the
car, and he came in.

My God! This man smelled good. "I have
to get this man out of my car for he is not safe," I
thought to myself. I found myself looking out my
own window trying to avoid making any contact

with him. He grabbed my hand, and I felt myself sliding down the car seat. He began to pray; I looked over in complete shock, then bowed my head to join him. It was now thirty minutes later. When I say this man prayed! He prayed!

We headed out of the car into the coffee shop. I felt so much better. That prayer was exactly what I needed. My mind was everywhere and now it was calm. We sat at the window in the corner of the shop. We exchanged questions and answers about where we worked, attended church, our goals, as well as what's important to us. We sat for hours talking about everything and anything. It was just refreshing.

Tonight, at our weekly Tuesday night service, Bishop is teaching on the Topic: "Life". He gave us seventeen Bible scriptures to read every day for the next 30 days.

- **Psalms 118:6**: The Lord is on my side; I will not fear: what can man do unto me.
- **Isaish 41:10**: Fear thou not; for I am with thee: be not dismayed; for I am thy God: I

will strengthen thee: yea I will help thee with the right had of my righteousness.

- **Revelations 12:11:** And they overcame him by the blood of the lamb, and by the word of their testimony; and they loved not their lives unto death.

- **Deuteronomy 20:4:** For the Lord your God is he that goeth with you, to fight for you against your enemies, to save you.

- **I Chronicles 28:20:** And David said to Solomon his son; Be strong and of good courage, and do it: Fear not, nor be dismayed for the Lord God, even my God, will be with thee; he will not fail thee, nor forsake thee; until thou hast finished all the work for the service of the house of the Lord.

- **Proverbs 29:5:** The fear of man bringeth a snare: but whoso putteth his trust in the Lord shall be safe.

- **Isaish 43:4:** But now thus saith the Lord that created thee, O Jacob, and he that formed thee, O Israel, Fear not: for I have redeemed thee, I have called thee by they name; thou art mine.

- **Genesis 50:21:** Now therefore fear ye not: I will nourish you, and your little ones. And he comforted them, and spake kindly unto them.

- **Psalms 27:3:** Though an host should encamp against me, my heart shall not fear, though war should rise against me in this I will be confident.

- **Psalms 23:4:** Yea, though I walk through the valley of the shadow of death, I will fear no evil: for thou art with me; thy rod and thy staff they comfort me.

- **Psalms 27:1:** The Lord is my light and my salvation; whom shall I fear? The Lord is the strength of my life; of whom shall I be afraid?

- **Luke 12:32:** Fear not, little flock: for it is your Father's good pleasure to give you the kingdom.

- **Hebrews 13:6:** So that we may boldly say, The Lord is my helper, and I will not fear what man shall do unto me.

- **Luke 12:7:** But even the very hairs of your head are all numbered. Fear not therefore: ye are of more value than many sparrows.

- **Romans 8:15:** For ye have not received the spirit of bondage again to fear; but ye have received the Spirit of adoption, whereby we cry, Abba, Father.

- **Judges 6:23:** And the Lord said unto him, Peace be unto thee; fear not: thou shalt not die.

- **John 4:4:** Ye are of God, little children, and have overcome them: because greater is he that is in you, than he that is in the world.

These scriptures came at the right time. I began to reflect on the last few days and how unstable my emotions had been. He taught about moving through life just functioning and not LIVING. He talks about how the majority of people on earth are dead and haven't been buried yet because of their unwillingness to live life to the fullest. He continued to give 8-key categories in which we should LIVE our lives to make it a little smoother:

- Establish Priorities – Be obedient
- Set attainable goals - always keep God first
- Budget Wisely – always pay your tithes
- Build Relationships – if you want a full life you have to build relationships with your family and friends. It helps keep a balanced life. Be open and honest. Practice honest conversations.
- Study Scriptures – know the scriptures to keep strength and to be able to fight off the enemy.
- Take Care of Yourself – find time to rest and let your body heal itself. Exercise. A body in motion. Stays in motion. Enhance your dignity.

- Live the Gospel – The Prophets have taught repeatedly that families should teach the Gospel. You're supposed to talk about the Gospel in your home as well as in church. Families will have eternal life.

- Pray Often – Pray in the morning. Talk to God daily. You should be convicted for not praying and having that relationship with God.

-Bishop Eric V. Jackson

CHAPTER NINE

I spoke to Nathan all week. He has been nothing less than a fresh breath of air. When I am with him, it's like nothing else matters in the world. He knew almost everything about me in such a brief period of time. He doesn't judge me; he just prays with me, and for me. I have never found that in a man in all my life living.

It was my turn to speak at our weekly group session. It seemed as if everyone was waiting to see what I had to say next. I was happy they were so fascinated with my story. Veronica looked at me and gave a nod, so I began:

Jonah was in jail facing charges of reckless driving, possession of a weapon, and domestic charges. He'd been calling me collect for a while fussing about going up to the prosecutor's office to change the statement I had made. I normally don't get police officers involved, but this time it couldn't be avoided. Victoria was done playing games with me. She was short tempered and easily angered, a bit selfish at times too. I don't know where she received that attribute from, but it was hers for the having.

Finally, I decided to give in. Nobody was going to take me to the courthouse after what had happened. My only option was to take the bus; it puzzled me I was riding on a bus heading to free a man who had literally put me and

his own son in danger. It puzzled me even more that I was riding a bus pregnant with a license to a car he crashed. I had lost the luxury of having a car temporarily because of him, yet it seemed all he care about was getting out of jail. I understood he was dealt a difficult hand in life; however, I just wanted him to do right by his son and me. We were bringing a whole child into the world. I needed to know if I could count on him.

When I arrived on the second floor of the courthouse, the court officer walked up to me to ask why I was there. I explained to him why I was there and what I wanted to do. After about fifteen minutes, a middle-aged woman came over asking to what matter I wanted to discuss with her as if she didn't already know why I was there. In a leveled tone, I expressed my desire to redo my statement to get the charges dropped against Jonah. She looked at me estranged as if she didn't understand what I was saying. I explained again. She told me that if I redid my statement, it would be obstruction of justice. I looked at her with a frowned face. She responded back to me with the same expression and ask is there anything else she can help me with.

I couldn't believe what she said to me. The nerve she had to tell me that I needed help, and I needed to use this time to focus on me. I left the courtroom abruptly. In my mind, I was preparing for the conversation coming up with Jonah. So many thoughts pondered through my mind as I took the two mile walk to catch the bus back home.

When I arrived at my parents' house, they were furious. The area where the courthouse was, wasn't the best of neighborhoods. It was near Thanksgiving, so darkness fell around 4:30 pm. Jonah called me collect that night. I told him what the prosecutor had said. I listened to him vent as well as blame me for him being in jail. Months went by, I gave birth to Trevor that April. Jonah was still incarcerated until about six months of Trevor's life. I did take Trevor to see his father a few times out of respect to him. After a while, Jonah didn't like me coming to the jailhouse with Trevor to see him. He didn't think it was sanitary. I agreed and we just waited for his release to have a bond with Trevor.

Jonah came home and I didn't even see him until about a day later. He told me he had things to do. Somehow, I knew what that meant. I just didn't want to go through that with him again.

A few years past with no issues. In fact, Jonah and I had moved and started to get along really well. He started going to church with me, reading scriptures, and even praying with me. I was so excited about this. We were putting God first and I was for everything that was transpiring in our relationship.

We were living together but were celibate by mutual agreement. I told Jonah how I felt about him. I told him I would understand if he didn't want to marry me just yet, but I had to do things according to God's word. I didn't want to force him to marry me just so we could have sex. I didn't want him to feel like I was giving him an ultimatum. Long story short, we were married that January at my parent's house. Victoria did such an awesome job making everything look nice. Although I wanted an actual wedding ceremony and setting, this was good enough for me. We didn't have a honeymoon because we couldn't afford it, but all was well.

Things were great for months until everything began to spiral out of control. My whole life changed in a matter of months, and I was not prepared for what I was about to go through. This test I was about to face would take everything from me.

Veronica looked at me as if to say, "that's it." I wanted to keep the suspense going. Besides, there were other woman who were eager to speak as well. It was time for their voices to be heard.

Octavia raised her hand to speak next. I grabbed my journal as she began to talk:

Hello everyone!

Lawrence and I always would get into heated arguments. Our arguments were mainly over the twins. I feel like things just fell apart after we had them. Don't get me wrong, I love my babies, I just needed more support from him. When bringing how I felt to his attention, Lawrence would always say I was weak. He threatened to take the kids when I would threaten to leave him. He never understood my perspective on anything. It was as if I was just in the relationship to please him.

There were many times I just wanted to pack the kids up and leave. I was just too scared to. It's hard to just

walk away after you have invested so many years into a relationship. He would always say he loved me. If he really loved me, why after five years, did he not propose to me? I did everything I could for him, and it just wasn't enough.

He should have felt lucky to have a woman like me in his life. To top it off, he was a perpetual liar. If the sky was blue, it was black to him. I began to have dreams about things he was doing. Genuinely believing it was God showing me who Lawrence really was.

He didn't understand the word "no' taking advantage of me every time he saw fit. I got to the point where I didn't want his dirty penis up in me. Heaven only knows where it had been. Lawrence thought he could talk and treat me any kind of way and I was supposed to just have sex with him at the drop of a hat. No sir, that's not how it works.

One time on the way to our family reunion, he was upset about me expressing my feelings to him. He threatened to hit me right before we arrived because I called him a lying coward. My family would question me about the contents of my relationship with Lawrence and I wouldn't tell them the truth. I was living a lifestyle where I thought nothing was wrong became second nature to me. Clearly there were issues that needed to be addressed, *however, I just figured it was a part of being in a relationship.*

Eventually, I had had enough, I couldn't take it no more. He didn't deserve his family. He wasn't providing, wasn't coming home, and wasn't engaging with the twins no more. When he stepped in one night drunk, I went through his phone and saw messages from his so-called new girlfriend. I called her and told her to come and get him. I was through. She came and picked him up; that was nearly a year or so ago. Recently, he reached out trying to manipulate his way back into my life. When he realized he wasn't about to play no games with me, he hung up. From then on, he has been blocked.

I have a good man now. When I first met him, I had a tough time trusting people. Things were a bit shaky due to my low self-esteem during that time, but he was so patient with me. Lawrence is not about to ruin my relationship with Miguel.

I wouldn't change anything about my past. If it weren't for my past, I wouldn't be the women I am today. I have come so far, and I have a man who loves me, and I love him.

When Octavia finished, I smiled. I genuinely believed the Lord had placed me here. It's irrational to think situations we face in life are only unique to us. Sometimes, we fail to understand that others are going through some of the same exact things we are experiencing. God really placed me with the right people at the right time. I was so thankful unto him. He knew the outcome of all of this before it even started. He knew I needed to hear other stories in order to not feel like I was peculiar. My eyes began to water as I thought about how good God is. Its amazing how much he loves his children. Who wouldn't serve a God like this.

(Jermiah 29:11: For I know the thoughts that I think toward you, saith the Lord, thoughts of peace, and not of evil, to give you an expected end.)

CHAPTER TEN

I didn't go out with the girls tonight; I was exhausted. Nathan and I were to meet this Saturday at the coffee shop like we normally do. I needed to make sure I was fit for that. This gal needed her rest for sure. Work had been a bit much lately. There were new policies and procedures being introduced. I just couldn't afford to miss a day or fall behind right now. I figured if I went to bed at a decent time tonight and tomorrow night, I would be ok to meet up for our coffee date.

Nathan and I were strictly friends. He respected me as I did him. I loved the transparency in him. We had the perfect friendship. It was him and I, no one else. There was no drama, no third parties; just a confidential, nonjudgemental relationship between two people who loved God. He was my lock box and being with him was such a safe place for me. I cherished every moment I spent with him. He's purity was a Godsend. At moments, I kept looking for something to be wrong with him. I would always ask myself; why was this man single, why did he want to be my friend, and was this just a season of friendship? I didn't know if I could manage loosing anything else in my life. I had lost so many friends in the past due to my choice to be with Jonah; I didn't want Nathan to be just a *season*. Having him apart of my life meant so much. In fact, it kind of stabilized me in a way. With him, I feel more confident about who I am as a woman. Nathann plays a positive role in my life and that's exactly the type of people I needed around me.

Dear Diary:

So much has transpired since the last time that I have journalled. I'm starting to learn who I am again. I spent so much time being a mom and wife that I forgot who Pheobe was. I guess you could say in the midst of all the turmoil, I lost my identity. Today, in devotions, I read II Corinthians 6:4-5,10: But in all things approving ourselves as the ministers of God, in much patience, in afflictions, in necessities, in distresses, 5. in stripes, in imprisonments, in tumults, in labours, in watchings, in fastings, 10. as sorrowful yet away rejoicing; as poor, yet making many rich; as having nothing, and yet possessing all things. I thought about how the way we perceive ourselves and our abilities are important. When the nation of people lived in Egypt, they were slaves and did not understand the power they possessed within by having God in their lives. We must not have an enslaved mind. We must have an attitude to defeat the enemy. Davids faith allowed him to have confidence in God. It doesn't matter what qualities you do or do not have. Davids perception was based on truth which allowed him to be an overcomer. Afflictions can oppress you and take away your identity as well as your performance in Christ, which affects one's ability to

*manifest in God. It's not just about guarding your heart
and emotions, but your body and soul alike. When your
body is afflicted, the heart suffers and attacks the mind
with anxiety. We have to learn to lean and trust that God
will comfort us in all situations no matter how bad it may
get. I believe this is where I lacked. There were times I
thought God had forgot about me. I was going through so
much pain mentally, physically, and emotionally, I
questioned God. I would speak to him, becoming frustrated
sometimes believing he didn't hear a word I'd said. But by
and by he was keeping me. The Nights, I hungered, he
didn't let me starve. The days I bled with tears and bodily
harm; he comforted me. The Nights, I tried to escape this
wretched world, he kept me. As I look back over
everything, I had experienced, I knew it was only through
the grace of God that I was still here and alive. The enemy
tried to break me, but Job 13:15 tells me, "Though he slay
me, yet will I trust in him". The Lord is sovereign and just
to forgive. I am so glad he has given me a second chance to
be someone's light in the midst of their storm. I count it all
joy. I'm not saying I have it all together, but I am so
incredibly grateful for everything the Lord has done for me.*

I went to bed with a smile on my face anticipating my early morning coffee date. I couldn't stand waking up so early, but it was for a great cause. At least, I thought so.

The next morning, I fulfilled my motherly duties and left to take my walk to meet Nathan. The sun was shining, and it seemed to be the exact type of weather from the first day I had met him. Nathan insisted on picking me up, but I told him I wasn't quite ready for that just yet. It was a bit different for me being a mother. Of course I had been to his house, I just wasn't ready for Nathan to completely see into my life.

On the way to the coffee shop the girls called to check in on me. I knew it was because I didn't go out to eat with them on Thursday. I told them I was on the way to the coffee shop; I wish I hadn't. They teased, teased, and teased me so badly. It was a sad case of high school drama for them and their curiosity about Nathan. I refrained from telling them certain things; quite frankly it was none of their business. What they did know is that I met him, but nothing more than that. Privacy is important to me. People sometimes can become too messy and overbearing. I had no room for that in my life.

As I reached the store, I could see Nathan standing at the door waiting for me. I smiled and told the girls I had to go now. They only let me hang up after promising to give them a call back tonight; I did and hit the end button. I pushed my phone down in my purse while Nathan grabbed my hand to hug me; being the gentleman that he is. We sat, talked, and laughed for hours. He asked me how therapy was going. I told him I opened up more, however, it was still pretty hard to tell a lot of what happened to me. He assured me it would take some time and that there was no time limit on healing. He also talked about how fear can place you in a position to not overcome what you're going through. He must have caught me thinking about what he was saying, because he gently grabbed my chin to face him. I had somehow become lost in the rhythm of the trees outside. "Pheobe, take that step forward, no matter how worried you are about what others may think of you, free yourself," he petitioned. It was the way he said "free yourself" that brought so many tears to my eyes. He came and sat to the right of me and wiped my face with the palms of his hands. I felt like a big baby. I knew my story could really help somebody. Our conversation brought me back to a bible study lesson Bishop

covered recently. We had been studying a book called, "The Assignment: The Anointing and The Adversity, Volume Two, Chapter 9" by Mike Murdock, which stated, "your tears today will be the rain on someone's desert tomorrow". Mike Murdock's statement has stuck with me ever since then. I told Nathan about this book, and he was ready to order it right in front of me. Sometimes I wish I had met Nathan years ago. I feel like we would have been so happy together. Maybe I wouldn't have gone through the things that I went through. Maybe my dreams would have come true. I started to feel myself shifting into a space of regret which I quickly corrected before he could read my facial expression.

Nathan and I finished our coffee. He walked me out of the coffee shop while asking me if he could take me home. I agreed. As we drove to my house, he began to tell me more personal things about himself, which I enjoyed. I knew he had to be tired of hearing about my life. He shared how he had recently lost his parents, which was extremely hard for him. I didn't have the words to comfort him, so hugged him as he drove his car. The conversation was cut short as we approached my house. He asked me what I was doing later. I told him, I was just going to tidy up the house a bit and watch a movie. He asked if he could join me for the movie. I smiled at him with uncertainty. "How about this? Let's have a movie night next week. You can come over and we can order dinner," he kissed me on the forehead in agreement, walked around the car to open my door, and watched me until I shut my front door. I stood their with my back against the door, "Lord, help me."

CHAPTER ELEVEN

Before I knew it, it was time for group therapy again. I rolled my eyes sarcastically at the thought of it. It's not that I didn't want to go. I was just so exhausted lately trying to keep up with everything I had going on. Working full-time, being a full-time mother, working on this book, attending church and its activities, and trying to have a social life was catching up to me. Maybe I should consider cutting my social life down some. Before I knew it, it was time to head out the door.

When I arrived at the session, it seemed a little different this time. The vibes in the room were a bit off. Everyone was a little hesitant and weary. It wasn't until I looked over at Veronica, I realized what was going on. There was a new woman in our group. It startled me because she looked like someone I knew so well, not in appearance, but in frailness. My face started to flush. So many emotions began to run through me. Flashbacks began to run through my mind with different phrases and snips of experience. All of a sudden, I couldn't breathe. I stumbled out the door almost falling when Octavia and Danille scooped me up out of the air to stand me up. Tatianna came directly in my face with a bottle of water and tissues. Normally, I wouldn't approve of people touching my face like that just cause some people don't care to wash their hands. But I was so out of it, I didn't even care.

The girls walked me to the conference room nearby to create a private environment for me. With Danille and Octavia still holding me up, Tatianna opened the door to the room to sit me down on sofa chair. It was big enough for all of us to sit on. What I admired at that moment was that they never asked me what was wrong. It was as if they knew. The girls sat with me, cried with me, wiped my face, and hugged me. This was something else I never had before. There was a pureness in their care for me. Although I had only known them for a brief period of time, these girls genuinely cared for me. Nearly fifteen minutes later, I felt strong enough to continue on to the group session.

When we all walked back in, Veronica gave me a thumbs up to make sure I was ok. I reciprocated it and proceeded to find my seat.She had waited for the girls and I to get back to start the session. I felt bad for having everyone wait on me.

We all sat in the circle as Veronica introduced the new girl to our group, Raina. Raina had a shy demeanor, she was extremely skinny, light in skin tone, with makeup covering her bruised faced. My eyes began to water. I began to go through my handbag to control my emotions. I knew she needed confident women around her to help her through this journey she was facing. In the midst of me gathering myself, Veronica called my name to continue with my story. For the first time since I started these sessions, I was eager to speak. I cleared my throat and began to talk.

Jonah had begun to engage with other females on the phone right in front of me. I knew he would be talking to a female due to his mellow tone. I would immediately confront him about it. At first, he would mute the phone, but after awhile he would cuss me out for confronting him about it. We would argue and argue in front of Trevor which was completely unhealthy for our son. Our arguments became so bad, he wouldn't come home for days. When he did come home, he would greet me as if he missed me. I would do everything I was supposed to do as his wife, even down to the bedroom, just for him to go back and lay under another female. After a while, I just accepted it. Jonah would always say "this" woman cooked better than me, "this" woman satisfied him better sexually, and "this" woman does more for him than I do. Somedays, I was so confused as to what I did for him to act the way he did; while other days, I didn't give a flying duck what he thought. I knew I was giving my all and if he was so unsatisfied why did he continue to come back.

I even helped him study for his state job that he landed. In return, I got nothing. I was still working, taking care of Jonah by myself, taking care of all the bills, transporting Jonah back and forth while he just ran wild with his money. Over the years, I didn't get anything, but a couple packs of diapers and a constant reminder of how the other women he was messing with were better than me.

I had been working and taking care of him for years. All those years prior, I would give him money to smoke up or invest in a new project he wanted to accomplish; only for it to fail. Never did I throw that in his face. Even when we entered into a marriage promising to be obedient to God, Jonah promised me if he got a new job, he would take care of his family like a man should do. This was the same man that came to God with me nearly a year ago in repentance. This was same man that did a 360 to treat me like a queen. This was the same man who made a

promise to be a father to his son, because he was robbed of having a father. This is the same holy man who was treating me worse than he ever had. I didn't even know who I was married to at this point. Time passed, and nothing became better. I was called out of my name consistently. He criticized everything I did from the food I cooked to the way I looked. He didn't like that I didn't dress like everyone else. He was right, I wasn't taking care of myself, but that was only due to depression from the way he was treating me. He would buy these other women things and take them on dates, while doing nothing for me. When I would ask him why, he would say that I tricked him into marrying me, which was far from the truth. I told Jonah before we were married that it was fine if he didn't want to be married. I just couldn't give him what he desired of me because of my choice to be faithful to God. He was making me feel as if I ruined his life.

Things were getting a bit tight financially. In addition, my mother-in-law was getting sick. I told Jonah I wouldn't mind quitting my job to take care of her to avoid her having a complete stranger come take care of her. However, I told him, if I were to do this, I would need him to take over financially. Momma Amora loved me, and I loved her. I told him it would be no problem at all to come and be of support to her.

Jonah agreed he would take over financially, so we moved in with Momma Amora. She was delighted and so was Trevor. They would get in trouble together sneaking snacks.

Throughout the week, I would cook for everyone, clean, take Momma Amora shopping, take her to church and to her doctors' appointments. Things became a little better for awhile which I liked.

One day, I left to go wash clothes at my parents house. I was going to stay the night, but something just didn't seem right to me. I told my father, Glenn, I wanted to go back home. We loaded the car up with my finished laundry and headed back to Momma Amora's house. When I pulled up, I noticed a strange car in the driveway. I didn't pay it no mind. "Maybe her family had come to visit," I thought. It was late though, why would they come this late? I unlocked the door and to my surprise Jonah was sitting there with Momma Amora and this girl. He looked shocked and mad at the same time. Glenn looked over at me and asked if I was ok. I told him I was good. He asked me did I want him to stay. I turned toward him and said, "Daddy, I got this!" It wasn't out of disrespect. I just wasn't about to let what they thought was about to go down, go down. I lived here. Nobody was about to push me *out of my element. I knew Glenn was in "protective" mode. I was trying to calm him, by showing him I was calm. Deep down inside, I was lit up like a BBQ grill. Glenn left after I reassured him, I was good.*

I looked at Jonah and asked him what's going on.

Jonah: What do you mean what's going on? Pheobe don't start with me.

I replied back to him, "Oh, we are doing this today!"

Jonah: This is Carey.

I replied, "I don't care what her name is. I'm trying to figure out why she is here."

Jonah: She is helping my mom. You can see my mom having a tough time breathing.

I wasn't about to let him have that. He could have called me. Momma Amora was on the nebulizer. Carey began to smack her lips in disgust. I looked over at her and asked her who she is.

Carey: I'm Carey, his girlfriend. I didn't know y'all were still married. He told me y'all were divorced. I would of never came here if I had known otherwise.

I replied back to her after rolling my eyes at Jonah. Carey, how long have you been his girlfriend?

Carey: Over two years.

She said it with an attitude like she was annoyed. I was asking her questions. I responded to her loudly, "Oh really, so we have only been married for a little over a year and you have been in the picture for two years?" Jonah became real defensive at this point. I was so irritated. The arguing persisted back and forth until I saw his mom gasping while even on the nebulizer. I apologized to her, and she said she understood. I told Jonah he was being really disrespectful because I live here. He stated he felt as though he wasn't being disrespectful because our area was upstairs.

I grabbed my laundry bag and took it upstairs. After all this was his mom house, I couldn't go tearing nothing up in here. Tears ran down my face as I started to put Trevor, and I clothes away. Shortly after, Jonah came upstairs and ask if he could have sex with me. I looked at him as if he were insane and said no. He grabbed my arm to turn me around. I argued with him, telling him he was trifling and wrong for what he was doing. I even asked him why he was upstairs with me if his girlfriend was downstairs. He continued to smirk in my face and try to kiss me. I told him if Carey is what he wanted, I was through. I was so tired of him. As soon as I said I was through with him, his smirk turned upside down and he spit in my face, grabbed my neck, and pushed me onto the bed. We were now wrestling at this point. All the other times, I never fought back. Today, it was going to stop. I was tired of being run over. We fought and fought, tearing the bedroom completely apart. He ripped my clothes off and pinned me on the floor and did what I never thought a husband could do to his wife. I had no more energy to fight. I was pinned and defeated.

I cried myself to sleep that night. Trevor slept at my parents house for the night, and I was so glad he did. My parents had no idea what I had been going through. I kept to myself and sometimes distant from them. Jonah began to mug me more often, point guns at me, threatened to shoot me off of the slightest things like looking at him. He would buy food for his mom, and Trevor, and leave me to starve. Days would go by when I didn't eat. I just cried. I would pray to the Lord and ask why I was going through this. Every time I would say I was leaving; he would threaten to burn my parents' house down or take Trevor from me. There were times where he would threaten to kill me if I ran away. I remember when Tre tried to come get Trevor and I, and he threatened to cut his head off if he came to his house. Tre had to cut ties with me off of Jonah threatening to burn his family's house down.

This man stripped me of my self-esteem. He had me questioning whether God really existed. I would pray and scream out in my car many days before starting my shift. I was choked, cussed out, spit on, mugged, smacked, raped, had things thrown at me, guns pointed at me, car windows banged out, punched, threatened, pushed out of a car, and more. I felt like a possession, this was not love. Everything I once did as a wife, I was no longer doing. He would never sleep at home anymore. I would spend nights at home hoping he would come back changed and we could be a family again. It was hopeless. He never showed. I eventually tried to move out only to get caught the one night he came home.

CHAPTER TWELVE

I stopped my story and gasped for air. It seemed I had been holding my breath. I looked around and saw a lot of the ladies with tissues wiping their eyes. Raina especially. Raina wasn't ready to speak tonight, so Veronica told Danielle she could speak instead. I grabbed my pen and notebook and saw Veronica whispering into Raina's ear. Whatever it was that was said, Raina nodded in approval.

I was never good enough. It always seemed like I needed to "be" more, to "do" more, often times, I felt like I could never just be me. At the start of our relationship, I assumed everything was sunshine and rainbows. We could finish each other sentences, we could go into the store and shop for each other, we could also even pick out each other's outfits without looking. It was almost like I was him and he was me. He was my best friend. Somewhere down the line, everything changed. I'm not sure if it was an outfit I wore, or maybe how I changed my hair, but something made him change who and what I meant to him. I began to lose myself and only wanted to be what he wanted me to be. I was doing things I would never have imagined myself doing, and next thing you know, I felt the only way to keep him was for him to have a baby with me.

He would say things sometimes and I would immediately start to come up with a plan of action to "fix" how HE was feeling. Unfortunately, that didn't work either. Eventually we broke up and I was so heartbroken.

It was the constant reminders of what I wasn't, that made me say, "hmmm, maybe if I did things this way, he would want me back". Well, that wasn't the case either.

When he found out I was pregnant, everything changed. One thing I can say is that while I was pregnant, he made sure I could never say that he left me "physically", however, the emotional support was not there at all. Many people fail to realize, "Living" and "Being alive" are two different things.

He was working late shifts, going in earlier, picking up second jobs, always finding a reason to hustle for our family and never be at home. What he didn't know was I knew that the hustle was in fact another woman. One day I began to call him, and he never answered so I started to follow his location using an app on my phone. After I couldn't figure out where he was, I tried logging into his social media, using any possible passwords I thought he would use. As soon as I logged in, that's when everything was uncovered.

I can't even say I was surprised he was entertaining different woman for the past two years of our relationship. I came to realize, before we got back together, he never had any intentions on making a family with us. It was girl after girl, after girl, after girl. When our son was six months old, I decided to leave him. From that moment on, it was like he was free. He had other girls in our bed that we shared, meanwhile telling me he wanted to fix our relationship. So, here I am again becoming another stereotype and raising another young Black man in a home without his daddy. This put me in a state of mental blackness.

I used to battle my emotions with alcohol and smoking weed. I stayed so high and so drunk that I was unable to tend to my children. I lost several jobs during this blackout. I remember my first Valentines Day without him, I was abandoned by my best friend at a party. I was so drunk; I drove myself to the beach to clear my head and was sexually assaulted in my own car. Even after that moment, I thought that he would care enough to come running to my rescue, but he blamed me for what happened.

From that moment on, I knew it was time I pick up the pieces, heal myself, and continue being a mom to raise my children. As the years went on, life got the best of me, and I drank more and more. My once lover became absent and never helped financially with our son. He would go weeks in between talking to him, which now created further distance between him and I.

To my surprise, my life was about to change again. Shortly after all this happened, I met my husband. It was nothing but the grace of God who delivered me from that attachment and allowed me to freely live in love. The love I share with my husband is unmatched. We just welcomed our new baby boy a few months back.

Because of everything I went through with him, I'm triggered by the actions of those around me and it automatically puts me in a place where mentally I am no longer yours, and you are no longer mine. I struggle with being in an enclosed space with men, because of someone who I do not know, taking my vulnerability and using it against me to harm me in the most absurd way. I do feel I'm always looking over my shoulder and trust is truly earned and not given.

I would say that I am finally in the acceptance phase of the healing process. I have accepted I have three children and all of them have different fathers. I have accepted that those who I love the most left me for the ones that cared least about me. I've accepted the new season that I'm in and I've accepted the growth that my life's journey has given me.

I do still maintain contact with my abuser because he is my son' father. At times, I will be in a room with him, and automatically feel triggered by certain faces he makes and certain things he says. It's almost like he draws me in. For five years he was my best friend, and that "time" just doesn't go away. With the help of God and the love of my husband, I am grateful I am able to move forward in life. My past made me who I am today. The only thing I wish I would have never had to experience was being raped. My past allows me to be a voice to those who won't speak up. My past allows me to continue to show that there is light on the other side and that the glory of God will shine through your life no matter what you've been through.

Danielle spoke so sincerely. She was such a loving person. When she cared for you, it was from the heart, and she had you; Octavia and Tatianna were the same. We all shared similar experiences. I believed that's why we connected so beautifully; these were my girls. When I tell you God will restore everything that you have lost, he will do just that. Everything I had lost before first stepping my feet into Virginia, had come back to me. Yes, I still had struggles. But God was right there by myside and has been by myside through it all.

I decided to go ahead and go out with the girls tonight. I wasn't up to it, but knew after tonight's session, we all needed to decompress.

We decided to eat a Longhorn. I ordered my normal baked potato soup with a side of Caesar salad. Nathan texted me briefly to check in on me and to wish me a good night. Smilingly, I returned a text. Octavia had asked me if I was feeling better from early. She stated she was proud of me for opening up the way I did. Tatianna proceeded in the conversation to ask, "What inspired you to open up like that?" I knew this was the million-dollar question everyone wanted the answer to. I replied, "Raina."

I saw myself in her. I knew exactly what she was going through just by looking at her. I told the girls she was going to need our support, and the girls agreed. "We need to support one another as well to make sure we are all healthy in the process of helping her," said Danielle. I agreed with her wholeheartedly. We could see that this girl wanted out. We finished dinner. I told the girls good night. I needed to go home, pray, and talk to God.

Dear Diary:

Today was filled with many emotions. Many of which I thought I had overcome. Nehemiah 8:10 came to mind which states the "joy of the Lord is our strength." As well as Psalms 16:11: Thou wilt shew me the path of life: In they presence is fulness of joy; at thy right hand there are pleasures evermore. I reflected on these scriptures. It was important that I didn't allow myself to dwell on what I had been through. They were not of me anymore. I was fixed on God. Redeemed by his goodness and mercy. There was no room for the enemy to present his self to me as if I was still a victim. I had elevated from Victim to Victor. I AM VICTORIOUS. Come what may. I know the Lord is with me. No more was I going to let Jonah control my present and future. I was moving forward. Everything that the Lord has for me, with his help, I am going to achieve. For I John 4:4 states that "greater is he that is in you, than he that is in the world." God has a plan and a purpose for my life. I refuse to let the enemy take my life from me. I have to live through the commandments of Jesus Christ. It was not about me anymore. It was about God.

Surely, I transitioned from journaling to prayer:

Lord, I'm thankful to you for allowing me to come into your presence. I thank you for another opportunity just to call on your name. Lord, I thank you for guiding me through this day. Lord.... there is something that I am about to face. Something only, you know about. Help me to get over my triggers so that I may be able to tackle this test that I am about to face. Also, Lord, protect Raina. This young lady is a lot like me. Give me the strength to be that vessel from you that she needs. I know she is my assignment. Help me guide her to you. Most of all help me to be obedient to you to not overstep any boundary or threshold you do not want me to go through or on. Let me be that light she needs me to be. Lord, help me please. I love you so much! I appreciate you bringing me through, so that I can be an inspiration to others that are going through the same thing that I went through. Lord, thank you for giving me another chance.

I stood up from prayer, laid down in bed,
and told the Lord thank you once more.

CHAPTER THIRTEEN

The next morning arrived, and I found myself lying in bed, debating whether I wanted to go to work or take the day off. After a moment of contemplation, I picked up my phone and ordered breakfast for everyone, then made the decision to call in sick. As I stood up, I could hear my bones crack, a reminder of how I had been feeling lately. Reaching for the curtain rod to let in some light, my phone rang unexpectedly. It was still early—8 AM—and I wondered who could be calling me at this hour.

I retrieved my phone from the bed and saw that it was Veronica. This was unusual; she had never called me before, which raised my concern. I hoped everything was alright.

"Hello, Phoebe, it's Veronica," she said, her voice tinged with urgency. "I'm really sorry to bother you at this hour, but I wanted to reach out last night while Raina was on the phone with me. Raina really needs help. She mentioned that when she first saw you, she felt there was something about you that made her trust you. She's not ready to share her struggles with the group yet, but she's willing to talk to you. She feels embarrassed and doesn't want her family to know. Thankfully, I was able to get her to a safe place; she's out now, and I believe her. I told her about you and your book, and she expressed a desire to help other women. What she really needs is someone she can trust, and I told her I thought you would be perfect for that."

After our conversation wrapped up, I felt a wave of gratitude wash over me. I was relieved to hear that Raina had found a way out and I was eager to help her.

I felt a sense of happiness because, while I was praying last night, I sought guidance for what

I knew was coming. God's presence is truly remarkable; the way He moves is both sweet and miraculous.

Veronica had given me Raina's number, and I was reminded of the biblical teaching that we are helpers of one another. That was exactly my intention. After gathering my thoughts, I reached out to her, and we agreed to meet for lunch. It was clear that the Lord was at work, and I felt there was a purpose behind my decision to take the day off.

I met Raina at Olive Garden, where we both ordered salads and engaged in light conversation. My goal was to approach her gently; I didn't want to overwhelm her, given everything she had been through. It was important for me to act with love and patience.

Midway through our lunch, Raina asked me how I managed to look so good after everything I had experienced. I looked at her and replied, "God." I shared that I hadn't always felt this way and that I had struggled for years with my identity as Phoebe. I spent so much time taking care of others that I lost sight of who I was. After I had come out of my own struggles, I faced years of triggers, reflections on the past, regrets, and embarrassment. It wasn't easy; I cried and prayed a lot, and I still do. However, I assured her that it has become much easier over time.

Raina looked at me with a glimmer of hope and asked, "It does get easier, though?" I reassured her that it truly does.

Tears began to fall down Raina's face as she looked at me, pouring out her emotions.

"Ms. Phoebe, this man has done so much to me, and I don't even know how to cope. I just cry. I know for sure I'm not going back to him. I called the cops on him last week, and they arrived just in time before he choked me out. I've done everything for him. It felt like we were married, but then something changed in him. I would ask if there was anything I could do better, and I tried to make adjustments just to please him, but nothing seemed to work.

He would come home drunk and lash out at our son, calling him terrible names like faggots, bastards, punks, all while blaming me. He said our son was 'soft' when he was just a toddler, and it broke my heart to see him cry whenever his dad yelled at me. There's no reason to call a child those names.

This man even peed on me just because I wouldn't give him oral. He has punched me in the ribs, threatened to rape me, and taken advantage of me with people he claimed were his friends when I was drunk one night at a club, thinking my husband would get me home safely. "I woke up feeling sore, exposed, and injured. He had hit me hard enough to give me a concussion. Despite everything he has done, I had still stood by him during all his legal troubles".

I looked at Raina, absorbing everything she had shared with me, struggling to hold back the tears I wanted to shed for her. She continued to speak, and I sat there to comfort her as she cried. I was grateful it was a weekday during lunchtime, and we were in the back of the restaurant near the window, where no one else was around. If there had been others present, it wouldn't have mattered anyways.

I looked over at Raina and said, "Raina, everything you've been through, I've experienced too. This is the first time I'm admitting all of this to anyone. I've always been so afraid to share too much, worried about how others might react. Just knowing that you're here, being so open with me—a complete stranger—gives me the motivation to express myself in my writing. I'm truly grateful to have met you.

Everything you're feeling is completely normal. I was kicked out of my own house while I was at work so he could move another woman in. He left all my clothes scattered on the lawn in the mud after heavy rain, and I remember crying as I picked each piece up. My mother had to buy me new clothes. He even used my car to take himself and another woman to work one morning while I was still asleep. He's broken my windows, and I could go on and on. There aren't enough hours in the day to share my whole story.

But Raina, remember that healing is possible. Don't let this man break you down. You need to forgive him, but most importantly, forgive yourself. You've already done the hard part. Let the Lord guide your steps—He is the only one who can make sense of all of this and lead you to a place of restoration. You belong to Him, not to anyone else. These men can make you feel like you were at fault, like you should have been a better partner, but that's not the truth."

I was told that the other girls did it better than I did. I knew he was lying; after all, why would he keep coming back to me after being with so many others? He still had a hold on me in so many ways, even years after I managed to break free. Deep down, I knew I had done everything I was supposed to do as a woman. Don't ever think it was your fault. I'm here for you, whatever you need." I took her hand and began to pray with her. She sobbed in acceptance as we prayed together. Before we left the restaurant, I told her she could call me anytime, day or night. She hugged me tightly, and we parted ways.

I felt that lunch had been a success. Afterward, I ran a few errands before heading home to see what my house looked like. Trevor could be so messy at times, and I never quite understood why. Other moms I talked to mentioned that their sons were the same way, so I guess it's just a boy thing. I took Trevor to spend the night at his cousin's house. When I returned home, I settled onto the couch to catch up on a show I had been watching. Before I knew it, I had dozed off.

Suddenly, I was jolted awake by the sound of the doorbell. I couldn't believe I had fallen asleep. I wondered who could be ringing my doorbell until I opened the door and saw Nathan standing there. Oh my gosh! I had completely forgotten about our movie night. He looked at me and asked, "Why does it seem like you didn't know I was coming?"

"Nathan, you know I can be forgetful. I really did forget. I'm sorry! Please, come in."

He stepped inside without hesitation and asked what I wanted for dinner. I suggested Chinese, and I told him he could pick the movie. I placed the order for food: vegetable fried rice and fried chicken wings, along with some Chinese Kool-Aid. I knew Nathan probably shouldn't be drinking that, so I planned to stop at 7-Eleven to grab him a Gatorade.

We started the movie before the food arrived, which ended up being delivered almost halfway through. It was a Friday night, so deliveries were understandably a bit slow. We enjoyed the movie, sharing laughs, and at some point, I drifted off. When I opened my eyes again, it was around midnight. I noticed Nathan was asleep as well. I sat up, and he woke up, asking what time it was. I told him, and he apologized for falling asleep, but I reassured him that it was fine.

We cleaned up the mess and I walked him to the door. He asked if I'd like to meet him for coffee in the morning. I nodded in agreement and watched as he got into his car before I shut the door. He was such a gentleman, and I appreciated that.

CHAPTER FOURTEEN

I met Nathan for coffee the next morning and shared that my book was coming along great. He mentioned he was proud of me, which was a sentiment I hadn't often heard from anyone besides my father. I found myself wondering why I hadn't met him sooner. Nathan then asked about my therapy sessions, and I told him I would be meeting again on Thursday, after which I would return to see Ms. Jane. We continued our conversation for a little longer before parting ways.

The following week passed quickly. I had a few conversations with Raina, and I was pleased to see she was doing better than I expected. I shared a devotion book with her that I had previously read, hoping it would aid her in her journey to Christ. During our last conversation, she mentioned that she had started to pray, and her son was even joining her in those prayers.

The time for the group session arrived again, and I hadn't heard from Raina that day, which made me anxious to see how she was doing. When I arrived, I found Raina already there, looking much better than the previous week with a smile on her face. She approached me with open arms, expressing her gratitude for my support. Octavia, Tatianna, and Danielle followed her over.

I had previously shared a copy of what I had attached in my story for the girls' approval, and Danielle had written her own story, so the notes I had taken were no longer needed. We sat in a circle as Veronica looked around the group.

She smiled and expressed how proud she was of everyone. Then, she turned to me and asked if I was ready, to which I nodded in agreement.

That night, as I tried to leave the house, he snatched the hamper out of my hands midway up the steps and pushed me down. He told me that if I wanted to leave, I could, but I wouldn't be taking anything with me— not even Trevor. I had purchased everything I intended to take, so I didn't understand how he felt entitled to dictate what I could have. Because I couldn't take Trevor with me, I chose to stay.

For the next two weeks, he remained fearful of my leaving and took every opportunity to insult me. One night, Carey came to pick him up, and he was taking some things with him. While she waited in the car, I asked Tre to come and get me, knowing he would likely take my phone. About ten minutes later, he left with my phone and some of his clothes. Tre arrived in his truck, and with the help of his friends, he loaded my things and took Trevor and I to my new apartment. Tre had had enough of Jonah. His previous threat to cut Tre head off was null and void now. He was determined he was going to make sure I was safe before he moved.

I settled into my new place and blocked Trevor, hoping for some peace. For a while, I didn't hear from him until one day he showed up at my door. I couldn't believe he had found me. He was calm and crying, apologizing for everything he had done. He expressed that he was tired of being the man he had become and wanted to return to who he was before we got married. I was naïve enough to believe him.

About a month or two later, Momma Amora moved in with me while construction workers were at her house, removing mold caused by a recent storm. I hadn't been feeling well for a little while, and after discussing it with my mom that morning, she suggested I take a pregnancy test. Sure enough, I was pregnant—Trevor was about to have a sibling.

As time passed, Jonah was treating me better than he had before, but something felt off. I don't know why women's intuition can be so strong sometimes. One morning, while making the bed, I moved his phone to the nightstand while he was in the shower. As I walked away, his phone dinged. Normally, I wouldn't look through anyone's phone, but something didn't feel right. I walked *back to the nightstand and saw a message from Carey. She was threatening Jonah, saying she would tell me she was pregnant. Apparently, she was upset that he hadn't been spending time at her place.*

Furious, I confronted Jonah as he stepped out of the shower, holding the phone up for him to see. He snapped at me, asking why I was suddenly looking through his phone. I told him I wasn't trying to invade his privacy; I just knew him too well. He snatched the phone out of my hand, and as I walked toward my dresser, Jonah had the nerve to ask if I was going to get an abortion. I firmly told him no—there was no need for that. I was his wife, and if anyone should consider it, it would be Carey.

He dropped the subject, but the tension between Carey and me became overwhelming. It felt as if she was the wife, and I was the side piece. She sent me a long, rude message on Facebook, and I responded politely, saying, "I'm pregnant too. I guess we're going to be pregnant together." I noticed the three little dots indicating she was typing a response, but then it disappeared. I found it amusing and exited out of the conversation. She never replied. Later, I went to Momma Amora's house, knowing she would be upset about the situation. As my pregnancy progressed, I found it increasingly difficult to walk. Jonah seemed to be more supportive, making sure I was okay and even keeping Carey away from me, even after she had their baby. I hadn't seen Carey since then. Jonah and I were trying to work things out once again. One day, I decided to check on him at his mother's house because I hadn't heard from him in a few days.

When I arrived, he snapped at me, asking why I was there and who told me to come. It was clear he was upset. I asked him, "Jonah, why do you treat me this way? I love you. I don't understand." I stood there, eight months pregnant, pleading with him for some understanding. He showed no remorse and looked me straight in the eye, saying, "I don't love you."

I responded in disbelief, "You don't love me? How could you say that? I've always been there for you, right by your side through thick and thin, and you don't want me? You're going to regret saying that. Anyone would appreciate my loyalty to you."

He stepped closer, his anger apparent as he spat out, "Nobody will ever want you! You'll never be anything! Get off my property before I shoot you!"

Momma Amora stepped in and began to confront Jonah, asking me to leave for my safety, which I did. About a week later, Jonah was locked up for violating his parole. However, he managed to get released a day before I was scheduled to have our daughter. Glenn called him and offered to pick him up early the next morning so he could be there for the birth.

When the day arrived, Jonah was nowhere to be found, and my father had to step in for him. Jonah eventually showed up after our daughter was born, smelling strongly of marijuana. I was in too much pain and recovering from the anesthesia to say anything. Afterward, Jonah took care of me and replaced my dad. He then announced he was going to Florida, claiming it was for a business opportunity. I later found out that he went to be with another woman.

Things didn't work out for Jonah in Florida, and he asked if he could return home to do right by his kids. I agreed. When Trevor saw his dad, he cried hysterically, *despite the way Jonah had treated him in the past. Kylie, only a few months old at the time, was simply happy to see anyone come through the door.*

As the months passed, Jonah became a bit aggravated, but it was still an improvement from the way he had treated me before. I found myself back in the position of caring for him as I always had. I was growing weary of it all. He wouldn't even watch the kids while I worked. I would go to work, pick the kids up, and come home to cook for all of us, while Jonah spent his days getting high and playing video games.

One day, Trevor came home from school with a letter from his teacher stating that he had brought drugs to school and that she would have to call DYFS. My heart sank. I called Trevor into the room to ask him what had happened. He explained that he had gotten into his dad's box that had arrived in the mail while I was getting my nails done.

I went into the room and looked under the bed, where I found a box containing drugs hidden inside pens. To make matters worse, the package was from someone in Florida and addressed to me. I was furious. I quickly gathered the kids and headed to the police station, determined to explain the situation. I was not about to lose my children because of Jonah. I had been loyal, but there were limits, and my priority was my kids.

DYFS became involved, and I had to demonstrate that I was a fit parent. As a result, Jonah had to leave the house. That night, he returned home drunk. I heard him and then heard Trevor crying, so I rushed into the room. I found that Jonah had punched Trevor in the stomach for telling on him. I pushed Jonah away from Trevor, while he hurled insults at him. Trevor was visibly upset.

In the chaos, Jonah grabbed my hair and yanked me away from Trevor, then pushed me to the ground and spat at me. I got back up, ready to defend myself. He then grabbed me by the waist, and we began to struggle. Jonah ran into the other room with Kylie, who was now crying from all the commotion. In the midst of it all, Trevor called the police, who arrived and escorted Jonah out of the house.

The next morning, I woke up feeling an overwhelming sense of dread. I confided in my dad, expressing my fear that Jonah might harm me. He advised me to come home. After dropping Trevor off at school, I learned that Jonah had picked him up. Concerned, I called Jonah to find out where he was, and he told me he was at his brother's house. I immediately drove over there, only to find Trevor sitting on the bed in the kids' room with Momma Amora. Jonah was waiting for me, fists clenched.

I demanded Jonah return Trevor to me, but he taunted me to "take him if you can." As I stepped into the room, Jonah grabbed my arm, bent it back, and pushed me onto a glass table. Determined to get my child, I got back up and prepared to fight. I was resolute in my decision to take Trevor home with me. Jonah swung at me but missed. I retaliated, landing a punch on his chin, which seemed to surprise him.

He grabbed my arm again, and as I tried to pull away, he swung at me and landed a punch to my face. I stumbled back, hitting the back of my head against the window air conditioning unit. Everything went dark and blurry for a moment, but somehow, I managed to get back up. Jonah's brother's girlfriend helped me get to the store to call an ambulance.

When the police arrived, I collapsed. They took me to the nearest trauma center, where I sat on the gurney with bruises on my face, an arm that felt out of place, a severe migraine, and blurred vision. I struggled to see clearly and began calling my parents repeatedly. Finally, they answered and rushed to the hospital.

I was fortunate to be alive. I stayed with my parents while I recovered. A month later, a judge recognized something in me and granted me full custody of my children, also putting protective measures in place for my safety. A few months after that, I moved to a different apartment, where I lived for about a year before relocating to stay with my cousin Brenda, Cedric, and their family. They welcomed me with open arms, and I have been living in Virginia ever since.

As I shared my story, the ladies began to clap and surround me with hugs, and there were sniffles echoing around the room. After the hugs, Raina looked at me and began to tell her own story. I felt a sense of pride for her. It was remarkable to see how my experiences had inspired her. She not only escaped from a physical adversary but also from a spiritual one.

CHAPTER FIFTEEN

After our group session, we all went out to eat, and Veronica generously treated us to the buffet. It was a time filled with laughter, tears, and prayer – a genuine bonding experience. I ended up getting home later than usual that night to my children. Trevor, my son, is a wonderful kid. He sometimes complains and can really test my patience, but for the most part, he's always by my side. Kylie, my daughter, is like my twin; we share a striking resemblance and have similar senses of humor, along with that introverted spirit that I possess. Overall, I truly cherish my family. Nathan has been a great support, offering parenting advice and engaging in meaningful conversations with Trevor when I need it.

Ms. Jane and I met that Tuesday, and she had received a report from Veronica about my progress. She seemed pleased with how I was doing. I shared with her that I had met a guy named Nathan, who embodies everything I want in a man, although it seems I might not be his type. We spend time together occasionally and check in with one another. Our weekly coffee chats on Saturday mornings are still happening, which I look forward to. Nathann is quite reserved and intelligent; we share that same "introvert spirit." When Mrs. Jane asked me how he motivates me, I smiled. I told her we motivate each other. She also inquired about Nathan's feelings regarding my writing a book about my experiences. I mentioned that he expressed pride in my accomplishments so far.

I shared with Ms. Jane a bit about Raina, explaining how she reminded me so much of

myself during my own struggles with abuse. In fact, I thought she was even stronger than I was back then. It seemed that my journey to find freedom had unexpectedly led me to build five meaningful relationships along the way.

At that moment Mrs. Jane looked a bit puzzled, but I chose to continue on with my thoughts. I told her how I had helped Taina gain control of her life through her faith in God. I expressed how I had discovered my purpose through my experiences and how exciting it was to walk in the direction that the Lord is guiding me in this season of my life. While things weren't perfect, they were okay.

Mrs. Jane continued to flip through the pages in my file, her brow furrowing with confusion. Concerned, I asked her if she was ok. She shook her head slowly and said, *"Pheobe, who is Raina? You've spent the last fifteen minutes talking about Raina, yet she isn't mentioned anywhere in your chart from Veronica."*

A wave of confusion washed over me. I replayed the last few weeks in my mind, but it all felt like a blur. I glanced back at Mrs. Jane, and as the realization began to settle in, I spoke in disbelief as, "Raina is me…."

CHAPTER SIXTEEN

Dear Diary,

When I first arrived in Virginia, I was utterly shattered. I felt like I was in pieces, unable to be touched or even engage in conversation. I kept to myself, unsure if anyone would accept me for who I truly was or merely as they perceived me upon my arrival. To my surprise, I was embraced with open arms. I joined a church and worked to fully restore my relationship with God. Yes, I made mistakes that I still regret, even after that restoration. Yet, God has shown me nothing but mercy, and I dare not take that for granted.

For years, I wondered when I would finally feel free. Today, I can say with certainty that I am free—no longer bound by my past or its lingering effects. I am deeply grateful for this program and, above all, to God for rewriting the ending of my story. As Nelson Mandela once said, "Forgiveness liberates the soul. It removes fear. That's why it's such a powerful weapon."

As for Jonah, we haven't spoken in nearly a year. He got married, had a child, and then seemed to vanish. No one knew where he went. There were moments when he tried to reconcile with me, but each time, he revealed the turmoil he still carried within. I've searched for him a few times, hoping to find some insight into his life, but I found nothing.

To Jonah:

All I ever did was love you. You broke me into pieces I'm not sure I can ever recover from. For all the many times you yelled, calling me out of my name, I forgive you. For all times you smacked me, I forgive you. For all the times you punched me, I forgive you. For all the times you pushed me towards the floor, I forgive you. For all the times you spit in my face, I forgive you. For all the times I tried to dress nicely to impress you and you either laughed or compared me to another female, I forgive you. For all the times you said you didn't want me, but wouldn't let me go, I forgive you. For all the times I cooked for you, and you complained my food wasn't as good as the other females, I forgive you. For all the times you took my car and banged my windows out, I forgive you. For all the money you took from me, I forgive you. For all the manipulation and confusion, I forgive you. For verbally and physically abusing our son, I forgive you. For cheating repeatedly, I forgive you. For giving me a concussion, I forgive you. For dislocating my arm, I forgive you. For the jobs you made me lose, I forgive you. For trying to frame me with drugs, I forgive you. For threatening my family, I forgive you. For trying to pimp me out, I forgive you. For urinating on me, I forgive you. For exploiting sexual videos I had no idea you taped, I forgive you. For raping me, I forgive you. For pointing guns at me threatening to kill me, I forgive you. And for every time, I tried to pray, and you bickered over me thinking that God didn't hear me, Shame on you! For today, I stand, after you told me, no one would ever want me, and I would never be anything; I am an author, a business owner, I am loved by people who knew nothing of me when I came to Virginia. God wants me, he is using me in a miraculous way for his glory. Every time I prayed; he heard me. Every tear I shed; he heard it. Every wind I spoke to, he heard it. All the cries and screams of pain, God heard it. I am everything you said I wouldn't be, and more…

I never claimed to be perfect, but I was loyal.

Just know… for every time……

I FORGIVE YOU!

Acknowledgments

I would like to express my heartfelt gratitude to everyone who has supported me on my healing journey. To my family, church community, and friends, your love means the world to me. A special thank you to Olivia Cooper for dedicating her time to design the front and back cover of this book; your talent is truly remarkable. I also want to extend my appreciation to Nick Woodson for the fantastic back cover photo from his professional photography work. A big shout out to his wife, La'Brea Woodson, for the beautiful hair styling that made the photo shoot a success. I am deeply grateful for the women who shared their stories with me; your courage is inspiring. To my children, Mia, and Jaydin, thank you for your patience and understanding. To my therapist, I appreciate your unwavering support as we navigated this process together. To my parents, I am thankful for your constant encouragement and support, especially when I finally opened up about my struggles. Your belief in made all the difference. To everyone who has offered kind words or assistance along the way, thank you from the bottom of my heart. I am truly grateful for each and every one of you!

<u>Survive</u>

For I have faced many storms,

traveled down countless roads,

been knocked down,

Cursed,

worn out mentally,

torn apart emotionally,

taken advantage of physically,

dragged through the mud,

and manipulated,

Yet Through the Grace of God, I have lived!

I have been lied to,

physically harmed,

cheated on,

set up,

threatened,

spit on,

and knocked down again and again,

Yet though the grace of God, I still live!

I have survived what was meant to destroy me,

overcame what many have not,

and endured because there is more for me.

No matter how many times you are knocked
down,

survive on purpose!

There is a God who sits high and looks low.

for all great things come from Him,

Live, I say, Live!

References

Holy Bible: King James Version

Jackson, B. E. (2024, September 8). Second
   Chance. (T. Marie, Interviewer)

Murdovk, M. (1996). *The Assignment: The
   Annointing and The Adversity.* Fort Worth:
   The Wisdom Center; 1st edition .